The Berkshire Studies in European History

GENERAL EDITORS

RICHARD A. NEWHALL
LAURENCE B. PACKARD
SIDNEY R. PACKARD

Berkshire Studies in European History

Under the Editorship of
Richard A. Newhall, Laurence B. Packard
and Sidney R. Packard

THE CRUSADES
RICHARD A. NEWHALL, *Williams College*
EUROPE AND THE CHURCH UNDER INNOCENT III
SIDNEY R. PACKARD, *Smith College*
THE COMMERCIAL REVOLUTION
LAURENCE B. PACKARD, *Amherst College*
THE INDUSTRIAL REVOLUTION
FREDERICK C. DIETZ, *University of Illinois*
GEOGRAPHICAL BASIS OF EUROPEAN HISTORY
J. K. WRIGHT, *American Geographical Society*
THE ENLIGHTENED DESPOTS
GEOFFREY BRUUN, *New York University*
ORGANIZATION OF MEDIEVAL CHRISTIANITY
SUMMERFIELD BALDWIN, *Western Reserve University*
THE AGE OF LOUIS XIV
LAURENCE B. PACKARD, *Amherst College*
THE SECOND HUNDRED YEARS WAR, 1689-1815
ARTHUR H. BUFFINTON, *Williams College*
IMPERIALISM AND NATIONALISM IN THE FAR EAST
DAVID E. OWEN, *Yale University*
EUROPEAN IMPERIALISM IN AFRICA
HALFORD L. HOSKINS, *Tufts College*
THE BRITISH EMPIRE-COMMONWEALTH
REGINALD G. TROTTER, *Queen's University*
MEDIEVAL SLAVDOM AND THE RISE OF RUSSIA
FRANK NOWAK, *Boston University*
IMPERIAL SPAIN
EDWARD DWIGHT SALMON, *Amherst College*
THE CHURCH IN THE ROMAN EMPIRE
ERWIN R. GOODENOUGH, *Yale University*
NATIONALISM IN THE BALKANS, 1800-1930
W. M. GEWEHR, *American University*
IMPERIAL RUSSIA, 1801-1917
M. KARPOVICH, *Harvard University*
THE RUSSIAN REVOLUTION, 1917-1931
GEORGE VERNADSKY, *Yale University*
THE FRENCH REVOLUTION, 1789-1799
LEO GERSHOY, *Long Island University*
THE AGE OF METTERNICH, 1814-1848
ARTHUR MAY, *University of Rochester*
A HISTORY OF GEOGRAPHICAL DISCOVERY, 1400-1800
JAMES E. GILLESPIE, *Pennsylvania State College*
CALVINISM AND THE RELIGIOUS WARS
FRANKLIN C. PALM, *University of California*
TRIPLE ALLIANCE AND TRIPLE ENTENTE
BERNADOTTE E. SCHMITT, *University of Chicago*
MEDIEVAL AGRARIAN ECONOMY
N. NEILSON, *Mt. Holyoke College*
BUSINESS IN THE MIDDLE AGES
SUMMERFIELD BALDWIN, *Western Reserve University*
THE RISE OF BRANDENBURG-PRUSSIA TO 1786
SIDNEY B. FAY, *Harvard University*
GERMANY SINCE 1918
FREDERICK L. SCHUMAN, *Williams College*
THE RENAISSANCE
W. K. FERGUSON, *New York University*

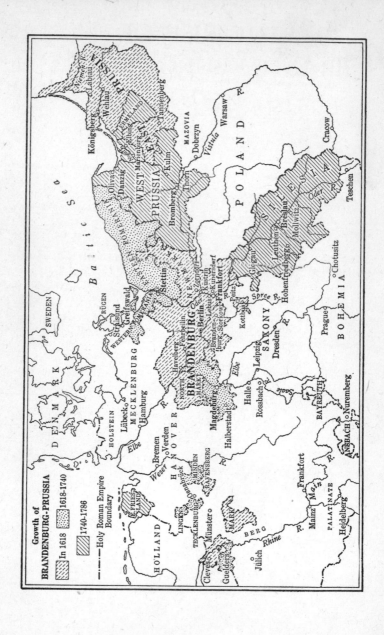

Growth of BRANDENBURG-PRUSSIA

In 1618
1618–1740
1740–1786
----- Holy Roman Empire Boundary

THE RISE OF
BRANDENBURG-PRUSSIA
TO 1786

BY

SIDNEY BRADSHAW FAY

PROFESSOR OF HISTORY
HARVARD UNIVERSITY AND RADCLIFFE COLLEGE

NEW YORK
HENRY HOLT AND COMPANY

PRINTED IN THE
UNITED STATES OF AMERICA

PREFACE

The college teacher of general European history is always confronted with the task of finding adequate reading for his classes which is neither too specialized and technical nor too elementary. For many topics, including several of the greatest importance, no such material is at the moment available. Moreover, in too many instances, good reading which undeniably does exist is in the form of a chapter in a larger work and is therefore too expensive for adoption as required reading under normal conditions.

The Berkshire Studies in European History have been planned to meet this situation. The topics selected for treatment are those on which there is no easily accessible reading of appropriate length adequate for the needs of a course in general European history. The authors, all experienced teachers, are in nearly every instance actively engaged in the class room and intimately acquainted with its problems. They will avoid a merely elementary presentation of facts, giving instead an interpretive discussion suited to the more mature point of view of college students.

No pretense is made, of course, that these *Studies* are contributions to historical literature in the scholarly sense. Each author, nevertheless, is sufficiently a specialist in the period of which he writes to be familiar with the sources and to have used the latest scholarly contributions to his subject. In order that those who desire to read further on any topic may have some guidance short bibliographies of works in western European languages are given, with particular attention to books of recent date.

Each *Study* is designed as a week's reading. The division into three approximately equal chapters, many of them self-contained and each suitable for one day's assignment, should make the series as a whole easily adaptable to the present needs of college classes. The editors have attempted at every point to maintain and emphasize this fundamental flexibility.

Maps and diagrams will occasionally be furnished with the text when specially needed but a good historical atlas, such as that of Shepherd, is presupposed throughout.

R. A. N.
L. B. P.
S. R. P.

CONTENTS

THE RISE OF
BRANDENBURG-PRUSSIA
TO 1786

HOHENZOLLERN RULERS

Conrad, Burggraf of Nuremberg, about 1170

FREDERICK I, Elector of Brandenburg, Burggraf,
(1417-1440)   and ruler of Ansbach and Bayreuth

FREDERICK II, "Iron Tooth"   ALBERT ACHILLES
(1440-1470)   (1470-1486)

(Brandenburg line)   (Ansbach line)   (Bayreuth line)

JOHN CICERO   Frederick   Sigismund
(1486-1499)

JOACHIM I   Albert,   Frederick   Albert, Grandmaster, 1511
(1499-1535)   Card. Archb.   Duke of PRUSSIA, 1525-68
               of Mainz

JOACHIM II   Albert Frederick = Mary Eleanor of
(1535-1571)   CLEVES-
                                                JÜLICH
JOHN GEORGE
(1571-1598)

JOACHIM FREDERICK
(1598-1608)

JOHN SIGISMUND = Anna   William the Silent
(1608-1619)   of Orange

        GEORGE WILLIAM   Frederick Henry
        (1619-1640)

    FREDERICK WILLIAM, the Great Elector = Louise Henrietta
    (1640-1688)

                                        Elector of Hanover

FREDERICK III (1688-1713) = Sophie Charlotte   George I
(FREDERICK I, King of Prussia, 1701-1713)   of England

    FREDERICK WILLIAM I = Sophia Dorothea
    (1713-1740)

FREDERICK II, the Great   Augustus William   Henry
(1740-1786)   d. 1758   d. 1802

CHAPTER I

GATHERING THE LANDS, 1134-1640

IMAGINE three small streams, with widely separated sources and distinctive characteristics, which finally flow together to form a considerable river; imagine then that the river in turn is continually joined by fresh branches until, growing ever wider and deeper, it at last reaches the ocean as a mighty waterway inviting ocean liners. In similar fashion grew the Brandenburg-Prussian State. Three small separated territories, put together under a single ruler and joined with other lands, were united to form the Frederician State and the Bismarckian Empire. "From the Mountain to the Sea" such was the symbolic emblem of the Hohenzollerns on their ancient castle in the Swabian Hills near the Black Forest.

The three small territories, sprawling out in widely distant parts of Northern Germany, were: Brandenburg in the center, mainly between the Elbe and the Oder; Prussia in the east, along the shores of the Baltic; and the Cleves-Mark inheritance astride the Lower Rhine. After some five centuries of separate existence these three territories were gathered together in a mere personal union under John Sigismund, Elector of Brandenburg (1608-1619). His successors steadily added fresh lands and gradually welded them together by a process of centralization and unification. Under Frederick the Great (1740-1786), these consolidated lands, commonly known as the Kingdom of Prussia,

1

became one of the chief states of Europe. Under Bismarck, Prussia united with herself other German lands to form the powerful and prosperous German Empire—which collapsed in 1918.

Not by wars alone was this consolidation of territory and power brought about. It was in good part owing to the extraordinary character and the peculiar abilities of the Hohenzollern rulers. They were generally good organizers, economical and efficient stewards, and tolerant, enlightened princes. Furthermore, each of the three original streams of territory made its distinctive contribution, according to its character.

Brandenburg's chief importance, as was natural enough from her central geographical position, was that she was to serve as the core of the Brandenburg-Prussian State. In Brandenburg were developed the governmental institutions and economic experiments which were gradually extended in large part over the other lands as they were gathered in, thus transforming them into a single, more or less unified, organic state (*Gesammtstaat*), politically strong and economically prosperous.

East Prussia, the land of the Teutonic Knights, furnished eventually the great landed nobles (*Junkers*), experienced in war and efficient administration, and possessed of a strong sense of duty and loyalty. From them came many of the generals and statesmen who helped to make Prussia great in the past, and who have ever—even today under Hitler—formed a dominating element in the army.

The Cleves-Mark territories, during the period treated in the following pages, were made up of quiet meadows with lowing kine, and small towns with industries and commerce much inferior to those of the adjacent Dutch. But in the latter part of the nine-teenth century this region became blackened with smoking chimneys, noisy with gigantic factories, thronged with steamers and barges, and teeming with population. Through it flows the Ruhr. In it lie the vast coal deposits which have helped transform Germany from an agricultural into an industrial country. In the sixteenth century East Prussia and Branden-burg became and remained predominantly Lutheran, and therefore politically and culturally conservative; but a considerable part of the Cleves population be-came Reformed (i.e., Calvinist) and breathed a more restless, democratic spirit, and also brought the Hohen-zollerns a wider contact with the more progressive Dutch and French.

What was the early history of these three distinctive lands, and how did they become united?

BEGINNINGS OF BRANDENBURG, 1134-1417

Charlemagne in his wars of conquest pushed the frontier of the Frankish Empire eastward to the Bo-hemian Mountains, to the Elbe and Saale rivers, and even a little to the east of the lower Elbe in the Hol-stein region (cf. Shepherd's *Atlas,* maps 57, 80). In-stead of trying to extend his rule over the Slavic tribes beyond this frontier, he was content to establish at various places along it a Border Count (*Markgraf*) to defend it. One of the most important of these was the North or Old Mark (*Nordmark* or *Altmark*). Trading towns and ecclesiastical foundations gave some oppor-tunity for intercourse between the Teutons to the west and the Slavs to the east of the frontier; but for more than two centuries after Charlemagne's day this line

of the Elbe, Saale and Bohemian Mountains continued
to form a sharp boundary which ever after distinguished the character of the regions to the west and
the east. Even the storks recognize it: those to the
west of it fly for the winter by way of France and
Gibraltar to South Africa; those to the east by way
of the Balkans and Constantinople; experiments have
shown that young storks, born in East Prussia, but
liberated near the Rhine, will still fly by the eastern
route over Constantinople.

In 1134 Albert the Bear was given the rule over the
North Mark. He belonged to the Ascanian family,
which came originally, like the Hohenstaufens, the
Hapsburgs and the Hohenzollerns, from the Swabian
Black Forest region in Southwest Germany. The
Ascanians had also acquired lands at Anhalt and Bal-
lenstedt on the northern slopes of the Harz Mountains.
Once in possession of the North Mark, Albert the Bear
was ambitious to extend his rule beyond the Elbe.
In the course of a long and energetic life (he died in
1170) he conquered the hill-fortress of Brandenburg,
baptized and made friends with its Wendish prince,
and established a bishopric there. Pushing further, he
conquered as far as the Oder and founded bishoprics
at Havelberg and Lebus. The native Slav population,
known as Wends, was not completely extinguished or
driven off. Some of them were Christianized and "left
sitting" (*Lassiten*) as the lowest element in the later
agricultural population. Some survived as fisher-folk in
their native villages along the watercourses; even today there are traces of them east of Berlin in the
wooded region on the banks of the Spree (Spreewald).
Their existence is further indicated by the survival of

place-names ending in *itz, witz* and *ig*, like Lausitz (i.e., Lusatia), Marwitz, and Leipzig.

But the greater part of the Wends disappeared under Albert the Bear and his successors. They were absorbed or replaced by German "colonists" from the west, where the land was insufficient for the growing population. The Ascanians did their utmost to stimulate this colonization movement. As land in Brandenburg was plentiful in amount but poor in quality, peasants from Western Germany were given generously of it—sixty acres to a family instead of the customary thirty-acre holdings in their old homes. Towns and monasteries were founded. The new settlers began to build with brick instead of rough field stones and wood like the Wends. Better agricultural methods and better military organization made it easy for the incoming German colonists to supersede the old Slavic natives.

Albert the Bear and his successors were engaged in almost constant wars with his neighbors, but gradually added to the North Mark an irregular group of lands which came to be known as the Mark of Brandenburg. It comprised some 10,000 square miles (roughly the area of the present State of Vermont).

The Ascanian Margraves of Brandenburg, as a result of their geographical position, came to be stronger than any other princes in Germany, with the exception of the Emperor. In charge of a military outpost against the enemies of the Empire, they had a relatively large military feudal force. As they were fighting against the heathen, they constantly received crusading recruits. The bishoprics and towns which they founded did not hold their rights from the Emperor, as in the rest of Germany, but were directly dependent on the Margraves who kept a strict control over them.

The Margrave was the sole proprietor of all the conquered land, except so far as he granted it on feudal terms to his followers and the imported colonists. Though in the North Mark he was subordinate to the Emperor, in the lands to the east of the Elbe he enjoyed supreme judicial as well as military power. So it was natural that, as early as 1230, the ruler of Brandenburg had come to be recognized as one of the seven important German princes who had the right to elect the Emperor. This is indicated in the Saxon Mirror of Justice (*Sachsenspiegel*), more than a century before the rights and duties of the Seven Electors were precisely laid down in the constitution of the Empire, known as the Golden Bull of 1356.

The Ascanian family had been prolific. Tradition mentions nineteen Margraves, old and young, who met together on a hill near Rathenow shortly before 1319. But their fecundity was in a sense a source of weakness. Following the pernicious German practice of dividing the inheritance among all the legitimate sons, some of the Margraves had pitifully little land or power, though one of them always retained the dignity and rights of Elector. But by 1320, curiously enough, all the Brandenburg Margraves died out, though a branch line continued for a century to rule as Electors of Saxony.

With the extinction of the Brandenburg Ascanians, evil days came upon the land. Brandenburg passed into the hands of the Bavarian (Wittelsbach) family, which was engaged in a deadly rivalry with the Hapsburgs for supreme power in the Empire. The Bavarian Electors of Brandenburg cared nothing for the welfare of their new possession. They seldom came in person to rule it. It was merely a land to be heavily taxed and exploited to aid them in their struggle with the Hapsburgs. Many of the territories acquired by the Ascanians were lost to rapacious neighbors—the Priegnitz to Mecklenburg, the Uckermark to Pomerania, and the Lausitz (Lusatia) to Bohemia.

In 1373 the last of the Bavarian Electors, Otto the Lazy, sold the Electorate to the Luxemburg Emperor, Charles IV. Better days began. Charles IV made a kind of survey or Doomsday Book (the *Landbuch* of 1375), which contains precious information about the economic and legal conditions of the Brandenburg population. But Charles IV died in 1378. For a quarter of a century more Brandenburg was neglected by his Luxemburg relatives, who had more important interests in the Empire and in fighting the Hungarians and the Turks.

THE FIRST HOHENZOLLERNS IN BRANDENBURG, 1417-1499

A new era of prosperity, good government, and princely power began with the arrival of the Hohenzollerns in Brandenburg in the summer of 1412. The "Zollerns" are first mentioned in a document of 1061. Their ancestral home was a Swabian castle near the sources of the Danube and the Neckar. About 1170 a younger brother, Conrad of Hohenzollern, left the family castle to seek his fortune by the sword and served under Frederick Barbarossa. He was rewarded by being appointed Burggraf of Nuremberg. This made him the Emperor's representative, not in the Free Imperial City of Nuremberg, but in the central German lands lying about it. As Burggraf he exercised justice, collected fines, checked robbers, and executed the Emperor's decrees. Though the office of Burggraf conferred no land, Conrad and his descendants soon acquired, by marriage, purchase and conquest, two considerable Franconian territories: the lower land of Ansbach in the valleys of the Regnitz and a branch of the Main to the southwest of Nuremberg, and the higher land of Bayreuth to the northwest of Nuremberg with the headwaters of the Main and the Saale.

One of Conrad's descendants two centuries later, by reason of his Franconian possessions and his natural ability, became the close friend and most powerful supporter of the Luxemburg Emperor, Sigismund. He fought for Sigismund against the Turks at the battle of Nicopolis in 1396. He helped him suppress a revolt of Hungarian rebels in 1409, and received as a reward 20,000 florins. He aided in Sigismund's election as Emperor in 1411. In the same year Sigismund inherited Brandenburg, but was too busy with imperial matters to go in person and rule the distant northern Electorate. He therefore appointed his friend Frederick, the Burggraf of Nuremberg and ruler of Ansbach-Bayreuth, as "captain and administrator" of Brandenburg, and in 1417, at the Council of Constance, formally invested him as Elector forever in the lands which he had been ruling for five years.

Frederick I (1417-1440), upon his arrival in Brandenburg in 1412, found a defiant nobility inclined to question his authority, a group of strong towns allied with the Hanseatic League, and a peasantry more or less ruined by the misgovernment of the Bavarian and Luxemburg Electors. It was Frederick's claim to distinction that he changed all this. He broke the power of the recalcitrant nobles in vigorous campaigns against their castles. He conciliated the towns. And he began

to restore the prosperity of the peasants by protecting
them to some extent from the oppression of the Junker
landlords.   For the first time since the extinction of
the Ascanian line of Margraves, the Elector's authority
was again strong and respected.

Frederick I, however, did not spend all his time in
Brandenburg.   After restoring order and authority, he
soon left his eldest son, John, to rule in the Electorate,
and returned to his favorite Franconian lands and to
a very active part in the affairs of the Empire.   He
commanded the German armies by which Emperor
Sigismund tried to suppress the Hussite revolt.   He
finally brought about the negotiations which put an
end to the wars with the Hussites, by granting them
tolerant concessions: communion in both kinds for the
laity, and free preaching in the national Czechish
tongue.   He was a close friend of Aneas Sylvius Pic-
colomini, who sang his praises; and at the church coun-
cils he vigorously supported the papal claims against
the conciliar party   He even had hopes of being
elected Emperor at the death of Sigismund in 1437.
But his ambitions were thwarted by various circum-
stances and by the jealousy of the other Electors who
preferred to choose a weak Hapsburg, like Frederick
III (1440-1493), rather than a strong Hohenzollern.

Though Frederick I was best known to his contemporaries as a Franconian prince and Imperial statesman,
and never returned to Brandenburg after 1426, he had
nevertheless established the Hohenzollerns firmly in
the Electorate which was to become the central seat of
their power.   In his ability as organizer, commander
and negotiator, he was a worthy forerunner of the
Great Elector and Frederick the Great.   Without ex-

aggeration Emperor Maximilian's tutor could say of
him:

This prince was a model of morality and uprightness,
such as is seldom seen in so high a place. By the virtues
which adorned his life and by his zeal for justice, he en-
nobled himself as a true Elector and made the name of
his house famed far and wide in the whole world. For as
the morning star shines forth in the cloudy mists which
surround it, so he shone among the princes of his time.

Before his death in 1440, Frederick I divided his
lands. He arranged that his eldest son, John, whose
nickname, "the Alchemist," may explain his lack of
ability in administering Brandenburg, should inherit
Bayreuth, which was relatively small, but prosperous
and easy to rule. His second and more vigorous son,
Frederick, became Elector of Brandenburg. A third
son, Albert, called "Achilles" because of his Herculean
strength and incessant wars, received Ansbach.

Frederick II (1440-1470) dealt a death-blow to the
pretensions of the Brandenburg towns, and thereby
won for himself the name of "Iron Tooth." The fifteenth century was notable throughout Germany for the
efforts of the rising territorial prince (*Landesherr*) to
break the power of the medieval towns within his territory. Fortified and self-governing, with wide market
and judicial rights, and leagued together, Brandenburg
towns formed a kind of state within a state. In their
local self-interest they made gild and commercial regulations which oppressed the peasantry and weakened
the authority of the Elector. As members of the powerful Hanseatic League they contributed to the support
of the Hanseatic navy, sent delegates to the Hanseatic

legislative assemblies, and received in return the backing of the League in opposing the Elector.

In 1442 a quarrel broke out in Berlin between the patrician oligarchy and the disfranchised lower classes. Frederick II seized the opportunity to interfere on the side of the latter. He forced the magistrates to surrender to himself the keys to the town, the administration of all justice, and a plot of ground near the center of the town on the island formed by the branching of the Spree. Here he built a strong castle and took up his residence, abandoning Spandau near by, where his family had usually lived. Berlin thus became the political capital of Brandenburg. Living in the midst of its citizens, he was able to quell instantly any revolt, such as one that took place five years later. The little castle which he built was greatly enlarged later, and became the regular residence of the Hohenzollerns. Having thus become master in Berlin, Frederick II easily extended his authority over the other towns of the Electorate. Legislation by the prince in the interests of the whole Electoral territory tended henceforth to supersede the selfish regulations of the local towns.

Frederick II was less fertile in ambitious dynastic projects than his father before him or his brother who succeeded him. But with the aid of able Franconian officials whom he called to his side he proved an efficient and economical administrator. By his patience and prudence he added more lands to Brandenburg than any Elector for the next two hundred years. Taking advantage of the financial necessities of the Teutonic Knights in their Thirteen Years' War with Poland, he bought back the New Mark from them in 1455, paying 40,000 florins for it. The New Mark, half as large as the rest of the Electorate, stretched out to the east of the Oder and was to be an important link in the chain of territories which was to connect Brandenburg and East Prussia.

Frederick II bought from the Emperor the judicial and administrative rights over the Niederlausitz (i.e., Lower Lusatia to the southeast of the Electorate), thus achieving a triumph over the rival Wettin Elector of Saxony. In this same region he also secured the rule over the little Bohemian fiefs of Kottbus, Peitz, and Teupitz, with the expectancy to Beeskow and Storkow. These gave him a firm foothold in the upper valley of the Spree and good defensive outposts against Polish, Czech or Hungarian attacks. But in a war with Pomerania he was unsuccessful. Discouraged, and by nature pious and melancholy, he resigned the Electorate in 1470 into the hands of his brother, Albert Achilles, and retired to a castle in Franconia where he died the next year.

Albert Achilles (1470-1486) was already fifty-six years old when he inherited Brandenburg and thus united under one rule, but for the last time, the Electoral and Franconian lands. He was still, however, a man of extraordinary physical vigor and restless ambitions. In his youth he had won prizes at jousting tournaments, and had made a pilgrimage to Jerusalem—more for adventure than piety. He planned many clever schemes which gained for him the dubious title of "the German fox," but which brought him no tangible advantages. The only new territory which he acquired was Krossen. This lay astride of the Oder, south of the New Mark, and was a first step towards Frederick the Great's later conquest of Silesia.

In 1470 Albert drew up for his Franconian lands a

very interesting House Ordinance (*Hofordnung*). With its detailed account of his officials, with their functions and revenues and the policies to be followed, it gives an excellent picture of the German system of government which was beginning to develop from medieval patriarchal forms into the princely absolutisms of the sixteenth and seventeenth centuries.

Albert also perceived the disastrously weakening effect of the German practice of subdividing principalities among many sons. He therefore issued in 1473 his famous constitution (*Constitutio Achillea*) regulating the succession of the Hohenzollern lands. The Electorate of Brandenburg was now recognized for the first time as the most important part of the Hohenzollern inheritance; it was to go to the eldest son. If there were two other sons, they were to receive Ansbach and Bayreuth. If there were more than three sons, the younger ones were to become ecclesiastics and be provided with small sums of money until bishoprics could be found for them. Thus there would be henceforth at most three ruling lines of Hohenzollern Margraves, and if any of the lines died out its lands were to be united again under the rule of the Electoral branch. In accordance with this wise constitution, Albert's three sons took their respective parts at his death in 1486: John became Elector of Brandenburg; Frederick established a separate line in Ansbach, and Sigismund one in Bayreuth.

Albert, like his two predecessors, was buried in Franconia, where he had passed most of his life. But he was the last Elector to be laid to rest there. Henceforth the Electors lived, died, and were buried in Brandenburg, which they had at last come to regard as their real home and chief possession.

John Cicero (1486-1499) was really no Cicero. He had no knowledge of refined Latin, and, like most of his Brandenburg subjects, was innocent of any interest in the new Renaissance movement which was beginning to transform the intellectual life of South Germany. The ridiculously inappropriate title of Cicero which has stuck to him was not known to his contemporaries; it was first invented by a pious chronicler eighty years after his death. His reign opened a century of comparative peace in Brandenburg, in which the chief interest lies in the internal development of the Electorate.

JOACHIM I (1499-1535): THE ROMAN LAW AND THE LUTHERAN MOVEMENT

Joachim I was only fifteen years of age at the death of his father in 1499. According to the Golden Bull he could not rule as Elector until he became eighteen. However, he promptly rejected the proffered regency of his Franconian uncle, Frederick, and appeared in person as a full-fledged Elector at the Diet of Augsburg in 1500. He had high ideas of his powers as a prince, and was determined to show his people that he intended to be master. In two years he had forty robber-nobles decapitated or hanged. This severity not being wholly effectual, sixty-five brigands were hanged in 1525. By a strict police ordinance of 1515 he placed the maintenance of order in the towns directly under the strict surveillance of his central government and reorganized the urban police. Though hardly a shining example of morality in his own personal life—he kept many mistresses—he made genuine efforts to raise the clergy from their ignorance and immorality.

His most important contribution to his country was

the foundation in 1506 of the first university in the Electorate, at Frankfort on the Oder. Though intensely conservative and little imbued with the spirit of the New Learning, the university was soon a flourishing institution; it even drew students from other parts of Germany, as may be seen from the matriculation lists which have been published. Under Joachim I it remained a bulwark of Roman Catholicism against the rising tide of Lutheranism. It even conferred a degree upon Tetzel, the famous indulgence seller, after he had expounded his views on papal infallibility within its walls. Its most important influence was in the training of students of Roman Law. These jurists, like the *légistes* in medieval France, formed a body of able administrators and shrewd councilors ready to serve the prince in his efforts further to break the power of the nobles, clergy and towns, and make himself absolute ruler. Preferring the precise, written, and highly developed Roman Law in which they had been trained and took pride, to the indefinite, customary German Law, which was largely handed down by word of mouth and varied greatly from locality to locality, these university-trained jurists tended to apply Roman instead of German legal principles. They contributed to that extraordinary phenomenon, known as the Reception of the Roman Law, by which a foreign system of jurisprudence was imposed almost imperceptibly upon a whole nation. This phenomenon was not peculiar to Brandenburg. It was taking place throughout Germany in the fifteenth and sixteenth centuries. A great impetus had been given to it by Emperor Maximilian's decree of 1495, that at least eight of the sixteen judges of the Supreme Court of the Empire

(*Reichskammergericht*) must be "learned in the written law," that is, in the Roman Law.

Though Joachim I added no territory directly to Brandenburg in his own day, his relatives secured appointments which later greatly increased the Hohenzollern possessions. His cousin, Albert, was elected Grandmaster of the Teutonic Order in 1511, and soon transformed its East Prussian territory into a hereditary duchy for himself and his heirs; in 1618 this was inherited by the Electors of Brandenburg, as we shall see later on. Joachim's brother, Albert, when only twenty-four years of age, was elected Bishop of Halberstadt and Archbishop of Magdeburg in 1513. The following year he became Archbishop of Mainz, thus giving the Hohenzollerns two of the seven seats in the Electoral College of the Empire during the critical Reformation years. Family influence and imperial favor combined to secure the election of Hohenzollern younger sons in Halberstadt and Magdeburg for a century and a half thereafter (with a single exception), until the rich and extensive sees were finally incorporated into the Brandenburg-Prussian State under the Great Elector in 1648 and 1680 respectively.

Joachim I was one of the most determined opponents of the new Lutheran doctrines which were spreading like wildfire in Germany. He took a strong stand against the Wittenberg monk at the famous Diet of 1521, and tried to enforce the Edict of Worms in Brandenburg by threatening the direst penalties to any of his subjects who disobeyed it. He conceived a bitter personal hatred for Luther and believed his subversive teachings to be directly responsible for the great Peasant Revolt of 1525. His chief aim in his later years was to check Lutheranism. In order to create for his son, Joachim, a bond which should hold him firm to the Catholic faith, he chose for him a Catholic wife, Magdalene, daughter of Duke George of Saxony. Duke George had presided at the Disputation of Leipzig, and cried out, at Luther's admission that the Hussite opinions were not all wrong: "God help us, the pestilence!" But all Joachim's efforts could not prevent the spread of the Lutheran doctrines among the people of the Electorate. Even in the bosom of his own family the heresy made its appearance. His own wife, Elizabeth, daughter of the King of Denmark, turned Lutheran in 1527. Her husband's threats so frightened her that she fled at night from Berlin, and sought refuge for eighteen years with Luther's friend, Frederick the Wise of Saxony. Meanwhile Joachim's Franconian cousins, as well as Albert, Duke of Prussia, had become champions of the Protestant party. Even his brother, the Cardinal-Archbishop of Mainz, was suspected of wavering.

JOACHIM II (1535-1571): NEW POLITICAL INSTITUTIONS

Joachim II, upon the death of his father, was at once besieged by both religious parties to join their side. Melanchthon made several visits to Berlin and revived that early inclination toward Lutheran teachings which Joachim II had undoubtedly felt nearly twenty years before, after a personal talk with Luther. Delegations from his own towns and nobles came to beg him to adopt Lutheran forms. On the other hand, the papal nuncios and the Emperor sought to keep him firm in the old faith by making concessions of various kinds. For four years Joachim II hesitated, replying in noncommittal language that in the matter of the Christian religion and ceremonies he would still continue so to act as to satisfy his conscience, his honor, and his responsibility to Almighty God and the Emperor.

By 1539, however, his subjects became more clamorous. Even the Bishop of Brandenburg openly adopted Lutheran practices. A delegation of Berlin burghers petitioned that at the Easter Communion they be allowed to receive both the Bread and the Wine, as Luther taught. Joachim's most trusted councilors advised him that the time was ripe for the introduction of the Reformation in Brandenburg. Accordingly, on November 1, 1539, Joachim finally received the Communion in both kinds. The momentous step took place in the new cathedral just built at Berlin with much expense, which he adorned with relics gathered from monasteries all over the Electorate, and sanctified with the bones of his ancestors which he transferred from the family vault in the cloister at Lehnin.

Joachim II, however, did not intend that his adoption of the Reformation should lead to a political rupture with the Emperor or the Catholic princes. To his Catholic father-in-law he took pains to explain: "We have no intention of subjecting ourselves wholly to the Lutheran teaching or of introducing any innovations. We simply wish to secure uniformity of ceremonial and discipline in our lands and thereby put an end to the *disputationes* and *quaestiones* by which the common man is nowadays stirred up." He allowed his wife to remain Roman Catholic and have her priests with her. He did not join the Protestant Schmalkald League or take part in the religious wars in Germany. He remained in close political touch with the Emperor throughout his life, endeavoring always to find a peaceful basis of settlement between Lutherans and Catholics, such as was finally achieved in the Peace of Augsburg in 1555. He pursued a middle-of-the-road policy, keeping a foot in each of the religious camps, and sparing his people the sufferings of a religious war.

Joachim II's adoption of Lutheranism gave him increased powers and duties. The princely absolutism which his father had sought to establish seemed at first about to take another step forward. According to Luther's conservative principle, the ruling prince took the place of the Pope and became supreme head of the church in each of the German territories which adopted Lutheranism. So Joachim II, as *summus episcopus* in Brandenburg, issued in 1540 a long Ecclesiastical Ordinance, a part of which, as he proudly said, "I wrote with my own fist." It reflected his desire to stand well with both religious parties. While it emphasized some of Luther's fundamental doctrines, such as Justification by Faith, the marriage of the clergy, and Communion with the Wine and the Bread, it retained as much as possible of the old Roman ceremonial: the elevation of the Host, Latin chants, genuflexions before the Crucifix, and Extreme Unction. It provided Brandenburg with a confession of faith, a catechism, and a book of ecclesiastical discipline and ceremonial. Every one had to obey the new Ordinance: "If any one should be so obstinate as to refuse to conform to this very Christian regulation, we shall permit him, by our generosity, to go and reside in some other land where he can live as he chooses." This half-tolerant principle, that the prince was to determine the religion of his territory, but that those of his subjects who differed from him might emigrate, was in accordance with the famous adage, *Cujus regio, ejus religio*, which was finally legalized in the Empire for

Catholic and Lutheran princes in 1555 and for Calvinists in 1648.

By his Ecclesiastical Ordinance, Joachim II succeeded in winning hearty letters of congratulation from Luther and Melanchthon, and at the same time received from the Emperor a formal approval of it, at least until a general or national Church Council should regulate definitely all religious differences in Germany. But Joachim did not intend that his church should be bound to either of the religious parties or involved in their wars. He regarded himself as independent: "I do not want to be bound any more to Wittenberg than to Rome; I do not say, *Credo sanctam Romanam* or *Wittenbergensem*, but *catholicam ecclesiam*, and my church at Berlin is just as much a true Christian church as that at Wittenberg."

Joachim also sent out commissioners who made a careful visitation of every parish, taking an inventory of church property, transferring superfluous silver vessels to Berlin, and making proper provision for the support of local pastors and sextons. Like his contemporary, Henry VIII of England, he dissolved most of the monasteries and nunneries and some other pious foundations. He placed the administration of the three bishoprics (Brandenburg, Havelberg, and Lebus) in the hands of his relatives. This secularization of church lands meant the virtual disappearance of the clergy as one of the three political "Estates" of the land. Henceforth, the Diet instead of consisting of three estates, as formerly, was composed of only two, the nobility and the towns. The revenues from the church lands ought to have strengthened the Elector financially. But they did so only to a small extent. In many cases the revenues were turned over to local uses, especially to the support of schools, hospitals, and the local ministers. Like Henry VIII, Joachim II gave away a large part of the secularized ecclesiastical lands to nobles and officials; most of the remainder he soon burdened with heavy mortgages in return for cash loans. It made little difference that he had been warned by the Diet not to do this, and had promised that he would not do so. Within a dozen years after his adoption of the Reformation, he had lost the revenues from so many secularized lands that the nobles and towns had to take steps to help him redeem the mortgaged property, and so recover revenues which he need never have lost, if he had been a more economical business administrator.

In 1543 Joachim II completed his reorganization of the church in Brandenburg by the appointment of a permanent Ecclesiastical Commission (*Consistorium*) to assist him in appointing pastors and superintendents, hearing ecclesiastical cases, and administering the rest of the church business which had formerly been in the hands of the three bishops. This Consistorium, composed of an ecclesiastical superintendent, a Roman-trained lawyer, and two or three other officials, with clerks, a seal of its own, and a regular time and place of meeting, was one of the first governing boards which differentiated itself from the rest of the Household Administration and began a separate corporate existence with specialized functions of its own.

TREASURY, SUPREME COURT, AND PRIVY COUNCIL

In the middle of the sixteenth century two great constitutional changes were taking place in Brandenburg. The first was the beginning of the separation from the Elector's Household of new organs of central government through the division of labor of the Elector's Council (*Rat*) into three bodies having charge respectively of legal, financial, and general political business. An exactly analogous development had taken place three centuries earlier in France and England with the threefold branching forth of the *curia regis*. The second change was the sudden decline of the Elector's authority and the rise to political power of the privileged nobles and towns represented in the Estates (*Landstände*)—a situation which lasted for a century, until the Great Elector crushed the Estates and established his own absolute power.

In Brandenburg before Joachim II's reign, as in the other principalities in Germany, there had been a very close organic connection between the management of the prince's domestic household and the administration of the territory over which he ruled. No clear distinction had existed between the prince in his private capacity as patrimonial feudal owner of large landed estates with an extensive domestic establishment, and the sovereign in his public capacity as the political ruler of the territorial state. The personal interests and affairs of the prince were still inextricably associated and interwoven with those of the State. The idea of public revenues, as distinct from the ruler's personal private income, had scarcely emerged. The government of the territory was still for the most part carried on by the prince's domestic household officials, most of whom actually still lived in the castle with him. They ate in the same dining-room with him; at night they received candles from the same silver closet, and wine and beer from the same cellar with him; and they stabled their horses in the same stable with his. The very title borne by some of the most important political officials—Marshal, Chamberlain, Master of the Household, Manager of the Storehouse— were reminiscent of their originally domestic character. They drew no distinction between the domestic service of the Household and the public service of the State, for the Elector's Household was thought of as co-extensive with the Electorate. The Marshal, for instance, after a busy morning going the rounds of the stable, inspecting the saddles or horse-shoeing, would join the Elector's other councilors, and discuss in council high matters of state policy, or perhaps receive and negoti-ate with foreign ambassadors. But every evening he would descend to the humbler but necessary task of noting how many people had dined that day at the Elector's tables, how much food was on hand for the morrow, and what necessaries ought to be ordered. From the inspection of the kitchen or the reprimand-ing of a disorderly scullion, he might go straight forth to lead the Elector's army against the enemy or to negotiate a treaty in a foreign capital.

By the time of the reign of Joachim II, however, came the glimmering consciousness of the distinction between the private and public aspects of the ruler. As the Elector gathered more lands, played a more prom-inent part in German politics, and secularized the Church lands, the business of the Household was in-creasing enormously in volume, becoming more complicated, and needing to be sorted out and dealt with by specially trained officials. These were furnished more and more by the university students trained in the newly introduced Roman Law. They tended to displace the old nobles who were bored with details and with a legal terminology which they did not very well understand. To meet this need of specialization of function and division of labor, the Elector began to assign special councilors or other officials to handle special matters. Joachim II, as we have already seen, handed over ecclesiastical affairs to the Consistorium in 1543. The three remaining main branches of business—financial, judicial, and political—were gradually given over respectively to the Treasury, the Supreme Court and (after 1604) to the Privy Council, as indicated in the table at the end of this book.

1. The Treasury (*Kammer*, i.e., the "chamber," where the Elector's hoard was originally kept) consisted of three bureaus. (a) The Comptroller's Office (*Amtskammer*) had general charge of the administration of the Elector's domain lands. These provided his main revenues, both in the form of rents in cash, but principally in the form of grain, meat, beer, fire-wood and other produce in kind, which was either consumed in the district (*Amt*) where it was produced, or was hauled to the storehouse in Berlin for the support of the Elector and his Household. (b) The Exchequer (*Hofrentei*) at Berlin received the cash revenues from tolls, beer-taxes, millstone and other monopolies, and also the surplus cash revenues flowing from the sale of produce from the domains; from these revenues it paid out the cash expenditures of the Elector's Household. The Treasury proper (*Kammer*), later known as (c)

the Privy Purse (*Chatulle*), received the surplus turned over by the Exchequer above the running expenses of the government, and also various revenues from other sources.

2. The Supreme Court (*Kammergericht*), projected but not actually established in 1516 as is incorrectly stated in most books, was first actually organized under Joachim II. It sat in the Elector's council chamber at Berlin on Mondays, Wednesdays and Fridays, so that some of the judges might be free to sit with the Consistorium which met on Tuesdays and Thursdays. It served as the highest court of appeal from the lower courts in Brandenburg, and no appeal could be taken from it to the Imperial Court, because the seven Electors, according to the Golden Bull, enjoyed the *Privilegio de non appellando*.

3. The Council (*Rat*) dealt with all the remaining political and administrative business, and especially with questions of foreign policy. It was presided over by the Elector himself or by his chancellor, and was not at first sharply differentiated from the Supreme Court; some of the same men sat in both bodies, and the Elector reserved some lawsuits for decision in his Council. But in 1604 the Elector, Joachim Frederick, was faced with difficult questions of foreign policy: especially negotiations by which he hoped to make good eventually his claims to East Prussia, Cleves-Mark, and other territories. He felt that he needed the advice of men with more experience and a wider point of view than the narrow-visioned Brandenburgers in his Council. He therefore appointed to it a Franconian, a Saxon, and a Rhineland Calvinist who had been prominent in Cleves-Mark. The old Council, thus

enlarged, was given precise rules and an organization
of its own, and was henceforth known as the Privy
Council (*Geheimer Rat*).

DUAL GOVERNMENT OF THE ELECTOR AND THE ESTATES

This budding off of new organs of government with
specialized functions of their own at first sight sug-
gests that Joachim II was moving further in the direction of efficiency in administration and the establishment of absolutism. But his reckless extravagance actually brought about a development in precisely the opposite direction, transferring much of the power from
the prince to the Estates and establishing for a century
the divided and weak system of government known as
"dualism."

Until the time of Joachim II the Brandenburg Electors had been mostly good managers and economical
rulers. They had been able to live within their regular
income from their domains and their regalian revenues,
with occasional taxes granted by the Estates. But
Joachim II was recklessly extravagant. He gave away
money and lands to his favorite friends and mistresses,
squandered his substance on costly buildings, sumptuous feasts, hunting parties, tournaments and imposing
liveries. No less than 452 horses formed the train with
which he appeared to take part in an election of the
Emperor. At the same time he had to pay his share
of the troops for the defense of the Empire against the
Turks and to protect his lands during the Schmalkald
Wars, in which, however, he took no part. To meet
his expenses he borrowed money from the Jews and
others at usurious rates, and began to mortgage his

domains. As a result, within five years he found himself so hopelessly in debt that he had to appeal to the Estates for help.

Accordingly, in 1540, the Estates (*Landstände*), representing the nobles and towns of the Electorate, generously came to his assistance, but only at the price of important political concessions on his part. The Estates assumed responsibility for the debts to the extent of 850,000 talers, an enormous sum for those days.[1] In return the Elector promised "to undertake no weighty matter, touching the weal or woe of the land, except with the previous advice and consent of the Estates." He promised them a share in the government such as they had never before aspired to. He consented that the management of the debts which they assumed should be taken out of his own hands and placed under a committee representing the Estates. He also prom-

[1] The taler was the chief German monetary unit, but varied somewhat in different parts of Germany and at different periods in the amount of silver it contained. In the sixteenth century one mark of 233.8 grams of pure silver was supposed to be divided into 9 standard Reichstalers, each of which should contain 25.9 grams of silver and 3.2 grams of alloy for hardness. In 1667 Brandenburg and Saxony agreed to divide the mark of silver into 10½ talers, each of which contained only 22.2 grams of silver. In 1690 the mark was divided into 12, and in the eighteenth century into 14 talers, thus furthering lowering the taler's silver content and depreciating its value.

The taler of the sixteenth century was about the size of the United States silver dollar, which weighs 26.7 grams and is 9/10ths pure silver, but it had at least eight or ten times the purchasing power of the present American dollar. See F. von Schrötter, *Das preussische Münzwesen* (6 v., Berlin, 1904-11), and, for tables of prices and values, G. Wiebe, *Zur Geschichte der Preisrevolution des XVI. und XVII. Jahrhunderts* (Berlin, 1895).

ised to contract no new debts and to mortgage no more of his domains.

Joachim II, however, had not learned the lesson which this ought to have taught him. He was too much of a spendthrift to keep his promise not to borrow further. Usurious interest charges ate up the revenues which were diminished as more domains were mortgaged. In 1550 he had to appeal to the Estates again, and they agreed to take over debts amounting to 1,250,-000 talers, again exacting concessions in return. The same thing happened in 1565, when, after long haggling, they became responsible for 1,500,000 more. In spite of this assistance, when the old man died six years later, the Estates found that he still had debts amounting to 2,500,000 talers.

To raise money toward paying off the debts, the Estates agreed to levy taxes, the towns contributing a beer-tax and the nobles a land-tax. But the Elector had to concede that the collection, administration and expenditure of these taxes should be exclusively in the hands of the Estates. Thus, by the side of the Elector's Treasury and fiscal agents there rose up a duplicate financial machinery (*Ständisches Kreditwerk*), with its own treasure chests, accounting and disbursing officials, and debt obligations, all managed by agents appointed by the Estates and totally independent of the Elector. Some of this machinery lasted until 1821, when the last obligations were discharged. This meant a confusing and disastrous dualism in finance, which extended more or less throughout the government. The Estates eventually had their own troops, separate from those of the Elector; they even tried to pursue a foreign policy at variance with his. And they demanded a share in the appointment of the Elector's officials.

This division of control and duplication of machinery deprived the Elector of effective power in domestic legislation and foreign policy, and yet did not substitute in its place any such efficient government as that of the English Commonwealth under Cromwell or the French Convention under Robespierre.

The Brandenburg Estates never secured a positive right of legislation. They could only act as a negative force checking the action of the Elector. On each occasion when he and his successors asked for money, they brought forward long lists of "grievances" which they insisted on having redressed. From a social and economic point of view this was unfortunate, because what they demanded as "redress of grievances" was usually the confirmation of medieval selfish privileges or the granting of new rights at the expense of the peasantry in the country and the lower disfranchised classes in the towns. The peasantry thus became depressed into a condition of servitude. Instead of being able to commute their labor services into money payments and so secure some of the advantages of the general rise in prices in the sixteenth century, like the copyholders in England, they were forced to continue their heavy labor-services for the Junker landlords. Instead of securing protection in the Elector's courts, such as Joachim would have been glad to give them, they were left under the arbitrary jurisdiction of the oppressive nobles. The Elector's efforts to substitute more uniform weights and measures for the great variety of medieval local practices met with persistent obstruction. Almost nothing was done for education, especially after the antagonism between the Elector and the Estates was sharpened by the Elector's adopting for himself in 1613 the more progressive Protestantism of Calvin, while his subjects adhered to a rigidly narrow Lutheranism. That the selfish interests of the Estates did not triumph more completely at the expense of the Elector and the lower classes was only owing to the fact that the social and economic interests of the nobles and towns were often so opposed to one another that they were unable to make a united stand in their demands for redress of grievances.

This dualism of government between the Elector and the Estates, which began with Joachim II, lasted with little change for a century, until the Great Elector. He broke the power of the Estates, established the absolute authority of the Prince, and began the progressive economic and social legislation and the vigorous foreign policy which were to transform the weak Electorate into the strong Brandenburg-Prussian State. Compared with the first Hohenzollerns in Brandenburg, Joachim's immediate successors, John George (1571-1598), Joachim Frederick (1598-1608), and John Sigismund (1608-1619), contributed relatively little that was new in the evolution of the country. Instead, therefore, of tracing their history, it is more important to see how the two other lands, Prussia and Cleves-Mark, were gathered under their rule.

THE TEUTONIC KNIGHTS IN PRUSSIA TO 1525

The geography of Prussia somewhat resembles that of Brandenburg—sandy plains, lakes and sluggish water-courses, an inhospitable soil, and open frontiers. It differs from Brandenburg in having a long seacoast from the Vistula to the Niemen, with two great lagoons almost shut off from the Baltic by long narrow sand-spits. The German colonization of Prussia also resembled that of Brandenburg, except that it began a century later, and was carried on by a military-monastic organization instead of by energetic princes like the Ascanians.

The native population, the *Borussi,* or Prussians, belonged to a group sometimes known as the Letto-Lithuanian, or Baltic, group. They spoke a language which stands philologically between the Teuton and the Slav languages. From the fourth to the thirteenth centuries the Prussians had lived a harmless amphibious existence between the sand and the sea, following their heathen rites and occasionally selling amber to the peoples of the West. A few bold missionaries had sought to make converts among them, but had suffered martyrdom for their pains. With the Poles to the south and the west they had frequent border conflicts, until finally, in 1226, a Polish prince, Conrad of Mazovia, unable to conquer or Christianize them, called to his aid the Teutonic Order.

This famous organization arose during the Third Crusade, when certain merchants of Bremen and Lübeck spread the sails of their ships as tents in the Holy Land to afford a shelter and hospital to their crusading brethren. Like the Knights Templar and Hospitalers, which were organized a few years earlier, the Teutonic Knights soon came to form a powerful military-monastic crusading Order. But they were at a disadvantage as compared with Templars and the Hospitalers. Arising later, they acquired less power in the Holy Land; and being mainly German, they received fewer pious gifts of land than the two other Orders which were richly endowed all over Western Europe. The Teutonic Knights therefore were glad to accept the call of Conrad of Mazovia for a crusade against the heathen Prussians, especially as they were promised full sovereignty, independent of the Holy Roman Empire, over all the lands that they might conquer.

From the Polish point of view, this calling in of the Germans, if regarded in the light of later events, was extremely short-sighted. The Poles permitted the formation of a German state between themselves and the Baltic which cut off their natural outlet down the Vistula River. They prepared the way for a centuries-long national conflict which was to result in the Partitions of Poland and the bitterness over the so-called Polish Corridor after 1919.

Transferring their forces from the Holy Land and from Venice to Northern Germany, the Teutonic Knights sailed down the Vistula, establishing block-houses at Thorn, Culm, Elbing and Marienwerder. Within a quarter of a century they pushed through the sands and forests eastwards, and in 1255 founded Königsberg, named in honor of King Ottokar of Bohemia who assisted in the conquest. In spite of a violent revolt of the native Prussians, which broke out in 1261 and lasted twenty years, the Teutonic Knights gradually made themselves masters of the whole south shore of the Baltic from the Vistula to the Gulf of Finland. In 1309 they moved their headquarters from Venice to Marienburg on the Nogat, an eastern outlet of the Vistula. Here they built a magnificent castle, with dormitories, banqueting hall, armory, stables, and a chapel with a mosaic of the Virgin eighteen feet high. These were all restored in the nineteenth century and stand today as an imposing example of a medieval monastic fortress.

The hundred years from 1309 to 1409 were the

Golden Age of the Teutonic Knights. Young nobles from all over Europe found no greater honor than to come out and fight under their banner and be knighted by their Grandmaster. After conquering the Prussians, they continued crusading against the heathen Lithuanians and against the Russians, as Chaucer indicates in his description of "the parfit gentil knight":

> Ful ofte tyme he hadde the bord bigonne
> Aboven all naciouns in Pruce.
> In Lettow hadde he reysed and in Ruce.

German peasants were settled on the conquered land on the same generous terms as in Brandenburg. Towns were founded and given wide privileges of self-government; they soon joined the Hanseatic League and developed a flourishing trade on the Baltic. The Knights themselves grew rich and prosperous. In 1310 they conquered from the Poles Pomerelia in the valley of the Vistula, and in 1402 purchased the New Mark from the Luxemburg family, thus making a solid avenue of German territory connecting East Prussia with the Holy Roman Empire.

But even in the later years of the Golden Age the Order was being weakened by tendencies which were ultimately to cause its complete decay and dissolution. It always remained a narrow oligarchy of not more than four hundred Knights. They formed a selfish, soulless corporation, exercising monarchical power, but without any of the human traits which have made personal monarchs more or less popular with their subjects, especially if they were men like St. Louis, Richard the Lion-Hearted, or Henry VIII. The Order never called into its membership any of its subjects in Prussia, whom it treated with disdain, but recruited

itself from noble families in Germany. There was
nothing in Prussia to bridge the gulf between the rulers
and the ruled.

This gulf between the Knights and their German
colonists was increased by the selfish monopolistic commercial policy of the Order. It reserved exclusively to
itself the profitable amber trade. It fixed tariff laws
which benefited its own export of grain and other produce in competition with the trade of the Prussian
country nobles and towns. So the Order came to be
generally hated by the Prussian nobles, who looked en-
viously across the border at the great power and privileges enjoyed by the Polish nobility, and by the Prussian towns, which wanted to draw closer their affilia-
tions with the powerful Hanseatic League. This feeling of antagonism gave currency to the rumors that
the Knights had become degenerate; that they cared
more for eating and drinking than for spreading the
Gospel among the heathen; that they had more ledgers
than prayer-books; that at their rich and riotous ban-
quets, instead of observing their original rule of silence
at meals, their talk was of horses, women, and unseemly
stories. There was undoubtedly much truth in these
rumors. Wealth and prosperity, as in the case of the
Templars in France, had resulted in moral degeneracy
among the Knights themselves and in envy and hatred
among the people about them.

Joined to these internal causes of weakness were
two external events which further undermined their
power. In 1386 Prince Jagello of Lithuania married
the Roman Catholic heiress to the Polish throne, became a Christian, and immediately converted all his
Lithuanian people. As the Prussians had long since
all been conquered and Christianized, and as there

could now be no more crusades against the Lithuanians, the Teutonic Knights had no more heathen to proselytize by the sword. They had lost their main reason for existence.

Furthermore, Jagello's marriage united Lithuania and Poland in a personal union, joining together in a powerful state two peoples who had hitherto weakened each other by continual wars. The Poles now began to regret having aided in the establishment of a German state along the Baltic which cut them off from the sea. Border conflicts between the Knights and the Poles became frequent. Finally in 1409 Poland declared war on the hated Knights—and was assisted by the Order's own discontented subjects.

The war with Poland marks the beginning of a century of decline and decay in the Teutonic Order, which ended with its complete dissolution in 1525. The Poles gathered a Pan-Slav army—Poles, Lithuanians, Czechs, Ruthenians, and even some Russians —and advanced against Prussia with a motley force of perhaps 35,000 all told. Some of the wiser Knights, seeing their own weakness and the chasm of discontent which separated them from their own subjects, advised negotiations. But the majority, self-confident and feverish for battle with the hated Slavs, insisted on taking up the fight. Collecting their own forces, and raising a feudal militia from the nobles and towns in Prussia, they hurried in the heat of July, 1410, to meet the Poles at Tannenberg. Though outnumbered nearly two to one, they started to attack. In the midst of the battle some of their treacherous militia lowered their standards and left the field. The Knights fought on with desperate bravery, but were cut down and killed, or forced to surrender. The flower of the Order perished. What was worse, their prestige was gone and the antagonism between them and their own subjects had been revealed. As a result of their defeat at Tannenberg they were forced by the First Peace of Thorn in 1411 to cede Samogitia and Dobrzyn to Poland and to pay the enormous sum of 4,500,000 marks of silver as a ransom for the captured Knights.

In the following years two Grandmasters tried to introduce reforms, by restoring the old discipline and by conciliating the nobles and towns in Prussia by giving them some share in the government. But these Grandmasters were opposed by the Knights themselves and deposed as traitors. Nothing shows more sharply the degeneracy and short-sighted folly of the Order in the fifteenth century than this refusal to eradicate the weaknesses which had been partly responsible for the Tannenberg disaster. On the contrary, the Knights increased the taxes to pay the ransom to Poland and to hire mercenary troops to defend their waning power, and thereby increased further the discontent among their subjects.

The Prussian nobles and towns finally formed a league in defiance of the Order, and in 1453 appealed for help to the King of Poland. The Poles were only too ready to aid the rebels. So began the terrible Thirteen Years' War, in which Prussia was ravaged and the Knights utterly defeated. In 1466, by the Second Peace of Thorn, the Knights had to cede back to Poland the Vistula region known as Pomerelia or West Prussia, thus giving to Poland again a free outlet to the sea and cutting off East Prussia from direct contact with Germany. West Prussia was to remain Polish until Frederick the Great took it back by the First Partition of Poland in 1772. The Order was al-

lowed to retain East Prussia (except the wedge-shaped
Bishopric of Ermeland which was joined to a Polish
Archbishopric), but only as a fief of Poland. Henceforth every new Grandmaster upon election must go to
Warsaw to do homage to the King of Poland. The
Knights "must love those whom Poland loved and
hate those whom Poland hated." They could have no
independent foreign policy of their own. The Prussian
nobles and towns could always appeal to the King of
Poland for confirmation of their privileges against the
rule of the Order.

ALBERT OF HOHENZOLLERN, DUKE OF PRUSSIA (1535-1568)

Nearly half a century after the Second Peace of
Thorn, the greatly weakened Teutonic Knights sought
to regain power by choosing as Grandmasters the
younger sons of powerful territorial princes in Germany. They hoped thus to get money and troops for
aid against Poland. In 1511, partly with this in mind,
they elected Albert of Hohenzollern, grandson of Albert
Achilles and cousin of Joachim I of Brandenburg.
Counting on the assistance of his relatives and on Emperor Maximilian whom he had once aided in a campaign in Italy, he defied the Poles in 1519 and declared war. But he was disappointed in his allies, defeated by the Poles, and forced to make peace.

Meanwhile Lutheranism had begun to spread among
the people of Prussia. Albert himself became secretly
interested in it, though still protesting publicly his
loyalty to Catholicism. In 1523 he visited Luther at
Wittenberg. Luther advised: "Give up your vow as
monk; take a wife; abolish the Order; and make your-

self hereditary Duke of Prussia." Albert was silent for a few minutes; then burst out laughing. It amused him that he had been chosen Grandmaster to strengthen the Order, and that now he was advised to abolish it. Yet this is precisely what he proceeded to do. He entered into negotiations with his Polish overlord and secured his consent.

By the Treaty of Cracow with Poland in 1525, the Teutonic Order was dissolved in Prussia and its possessions were transformed into a hereditary duchy for Albert and his descendants, as vassals of the King of Poland. The treaty was approved by the Estates of Prussia. Albert then proceeded to Cracow, took the oath of homage as Duke of Prussia, and received a banner with the Prussian black eagle.

Albert I (1525-1568) began his rule energetically by introducing the Lutheran organization everywhere in Prussia and by showing a real interest in the Renaissance. He was the personal friend of the painters, Lucas Cranach and Albrecht Dürer, and of the sculptor, Peter Vischer. He founded at Königsberg a printing press, a library, and in 1544 the famous *Albertina,* or university. But in his later years he became indolent, fell into the hands of favorites, and was forced to make such wide concessions to the Estates, representing the Prussian nobles and towns, that he was stripped of a large part of his ducal power.

JOHN SIGISMUND (1608-1619): RULER IN BRANDENBURG, CLEVES-MARK, AND PRUSSIA

Albert's son and successor, Albert Frederick (1568-1618), had a long and miserable existence. Early signs of feeble-mindedness gradually developed into serious mental derangement; fits of moroseness and refusal to take food, for fear of being poisoned, alternated with a feverish fondness for gaiety in dancing and drinking and pommeling his servants. A regency had to be instituted, which was ably administered by his cousin, George Frederick of Ansbach, from 1577 to the latter's death in 1603, and afterwards by John Sigismund, Elector of Brandenburg. Albert Frederick's mental condition made it easy for the Prussian Estates to arrogate to themselves an even greater despotism over the peasants and a still larger control over the government than during the last years of his weak father. The Polish overlord was also always ready to favor the Estates at the expense of the Duke. So it came about that, whereas in Brandenburg the division of power between the prince and the Estates resulted in a kind of "dualism," in Prussia the government virtually passed out of the hands of the prince into the control of the narrow-minded and intensely Lutheran Estates, an unfortunate situation which was intensified after John Sigismund turned Calvinist in 1613.

In order to establish a Hohenzollern claim to territories in the valley of the Rhine, Albert Frederick had been betrothed to Mary Eleanor, eldest daughter of William the Rich of Cleves-Jülich. After she set out for Prussia, she learned of the mental state of her betrothed; but as she had twice been disappointed in hopes of marriage, she decided not to lose this third chance. She married the crazy Duke, and bore him numerous children, but only the daughters lived to grow up. The eldest, Anna, married John Sigismund, Elector of Brandenburg, thus giving him a claim to the Cleves-Jülich lands.

The Cleves-Jülich inheritance consisted chiefly of

five small duchies and counties: Cleves, Mark, Jülich, Berg and Ravensberg (cf. Shepherd's *Atlas,* maps 114, 122), inhabited by Catholics, Lutherans and Calvinists. Although not large, their fate, at the extinction of the direct ruling line in 1609, became of great European importance. If they fell to a Protestant, it would aid the Dutch in their struggle for independence against the Spanish Hapsburgs and strengthen the German Protestants in their struggle against the Counter-Reformation. If they fell to a Catholic, they would form an easy connecting link between the Spanish Hapsburgs in the Netherlands and the lands of the Austrian Hapsburgs in the Upper Rhine and Danube valleys. Henry IV of France, James I of England, the Dutch, and the Protestant Union, mainly composed of German Calvinists, were therefore inclined to support the Protestant claimants. The Pope, the Hapsburgs at Vienna and Madrid, and the German Catholic League, led by the Duke of Bavaria, favored a Catholic ruler. There was danger that the question might lead to a general European war.

The principal claimants were: John Sigismund of Brandenburg, a Lutheran; the Duke of Neuburg, a Calvinist; and the Emperor who claimed the lands as escheated fiefs of the Empire, and sent Archduke Leopold with an armed force to seize Jülich.

In the face of this Catholic danger, John Sigismund and the Duke of Neuburg pooled their Protestant interests and agreed to exercise a joint rule (*condominium*) as "Possessory Princes." With the aid of French troops, sent in spite of the assassination of Henry IV, they expelled Archduke Leopold from Jülich. But the condominium did not work smoothly. Friction between the Possessory Princes was inevitable. Hard words, after heavy drinking, took place between them. Though Carlyle's picturesque story of Neuburg turning from Calvinism to Catholicism because John Sigismund boxed his ears is pure legend, it is true that in 1613 the two men quarreled. Neuburg, finding little support from the Protestant Union in Germany, then turned Catholic, married the sister of the Catholic Duke Maximilian of Bavaria, and sought the help of his Catholic League.

Six months later John Sigismund turned Calvinist. Since his youth he had been favorably impressed by the Calvinists and their Heidelberg Catechism. Two of his best friends and wisest councilors, Herr von Rheydt and Abraham Dohna, were Calvinists and enjoyed close relations with the Orange family in the Netherlands. On the other hand, his father, his wife, and his Brandenburg and Prussian Estates were so vehemently Lutheran that he was deterred from an open change of faith until 1613, when his sincere religious motives were reinforced by the political consideration that as a Calvinist he might more easily get the Calvinists in the Netherlands, France and the German Protestant Union to back him in his claims to the Cleves-Jülich inheritance. Whether he was primarily actuated by the religious or the political motive is less important than the fact that henceforth the Hohenzollerns widened their political horizon westward by establishing closer contact with the more progressive Dutch Reformed and the French Huguenots, and ceased to be of the same faith as the great majority of their own Lutheran subjects in Brandenburg and Prussia. Consequently John Sigismund accompanied his adoption of Calvinism with the announcement that he would make no use of his right, *cujus regio, ejus religio,* but that all his subjects might enjoy religious freedom—a noteworthy example of toleration in an age of intolerance.

The Cleves-Jülich inheritance question was settled next year by a compromise: in the Treaty of Xanten of 1614 John Sigismund took over the administration of Cleves, Mark and Ravensberg, and the Duke of Neuburg that of Jülich and Berg; but both princes still reserved their legal claims to all the lands. Half a century later, in 1666, this provisional division of 1614 was made final.

In the east John Sigismund made an even more important territorial gain. At the death of the crazy old Duke of Prussia, Albert Frederick, and in accord with earlier family agreements, the Elector of Brandenburg became Duke of Prussia in 1618, and, as such, became a vassal of the King of Poland.

John Sigismund's reign, bringing Brandenburg, Cleves-Mark and Prussia under one ruler, gave to the Hohenzollerns the prospect of a brilliant future. The widely separated lands foreshadowed the future territorial outline of the later Kingdom of Prussia. It became the ambition of his successors to link them together by acquiring the intervening territory. The union of the three territories, to be sure, was only "personal," and not "organic"; that is, each territory still retained its own separate organization and institutions and tried to pursue its own local selfish policies. It remained for the later Hohenzollerns to transform the personal into an organic union, extending many Brandenburg institutions over the other lands, and thus creating a unified and centralized state, in which the single will of the

Prince was far stronger and more enlightened than the narrow separatist tendencies of the local Estates.

Hardly had John Sigismund succeeded in uniting the three streams of territory, when all Germany began to be scourged by the terrible Thirty Years' War.

CHAPTER II

THE REIGN OF THE GREAT ELECTOR,
1640-1688

THE Thirty Years' War (1618-1648), beginning at the moment when John Sigismund's union of Brandenburg, Cleves and Prussia had seemed to open such a fair prospect for the Hohenzollerns, caused indescribable devastation and delayed all organic reforms for more than two decades.

His son and successor, George William (1619-1640), weak, vacillating, and easily influenced, was not at all the kind of man to face successfully the trying times when Germany was torn by civil war and trampled upon by foreign enemies. In each of his three territories the all-powerful Estates controlled most of the revenues, yet would raise no troops, except occasionally a few for local use and under the command of their own officers. As George William had almost no available money, he could not hire soldiers; consequently he could command no respect and could have no effective foreign policy.

Throughout his reign George William was torn between conflicting factions. His Privy Council, containing Lutherans, Calvinists, and a Catholic, was bitterly divided against itself, until the Catholic, Adam von Schwartzenberg, managed to oust his opponents and make himself virtually dictator. George William himself was a Calvinist, and had married a sister of Frederick V of the Palatinate, the unfortunate "Winter

King." But his domineering mother, Anna of Prussia, and almost all his subjects were fanatically Lutheran, as bitterly opposed to Calvinism as to Catholicism. So the helpless Elector, caught in the storm of the Thirty Years' War, tried in turn three different policies— neutrality, alliance with the Lutheran Swedes, and alliance with the Catholic Imperialists—each of which inflicted untold misery and misfortune on his lands.

In allying with the Catholics after 1635, Schwartzenberg hoped to raise an army of 26,000 men, expel the Swedes, and make good the Elector's claim to Pomerania, where the last duke had died without direct heirs in 1637. In fact he was able to raise only 11,000. Even these were so disorderly and disobedient that they not only failed to occupy Pomerania, but were unable to prevent the towns in northern Brandenburg from being treated in terrible fashion by the Swedes. In 1638 George William, discouraged and suffering from an old injury to his leg, was carried in a litter from Berlin to greater safety in Königsberg. Schwartzenberg, remaining behind as virtual dictator in Brandenburg, had grandiose plans for weakening the Estates and building up a strong government in alliance with the Emperor. By the Elector's subjects, however, he was universally hated as a traitor and an agent of the Hapsburgs. Moreover, he failed to drive out the Swedes and had enriched himself, while the Elector and those about him were impoverished more and more miserably. His rule, however, was suddenly cut short by death on March 14, 1641. A few weeks earlier George William had also died and been succeeded by his son, Frederick William, an inexperienced youth of twenty, who was to win for himself the justly proud title of the "Great Elector."

THE GREAT ELECTOR'S YOUTH, 1620-1640

Frederick William was born in the old Hohenzollern castle at Berlin on February 16, 1620. From his earliest infancy there fell across his life the shadow of the Thirty Years' War. For months he lay unbaptized in his cradle, because there was no money for the baptismal festivities and because no suitable god-parents could be secured. At the age of seven, when Wallenstein's soldiers threatened the Electorate, he was transferred from the insecurity of Berlin to the strong fortress of Küstrin, and placed under an excellent tutor. Though always holding firmly to the Calvinist teachings of his parents and tutor, he respected, like his grandfather, John Sigismund, the religious convictions of others. His tolerance in an age of intolerance was one of his noblest characteristics, and incidentally was to prove of great material advantage to his country. He later refused to turn Lutheran to secure the throne of Sweden, or Catholic to secure that of Poland. It was genuine reverence and religious feeling, not weak piety or goody-goody hypocrisy, which made him at the age of fourteen choose as his life-motto the words of the Psalmist:

> Cause me to know the way wherein I should walk;
> For I lift up my soul to thee.

His progress in his studies was satisfactory but not remarkable. He showed good aptitude in drawing, geography, applied mathematics, mechanics, and languages. His first letter to his father, written at the age of seven and thanking him for a horse, was in French, which he learned to write and speak with ease. The

same was true of Dutch. He was given a couple of
Polish playmates, in order that he might learn more
easily the language of his future Polish overlord. He
early developed a hobby for collecting books, engrav-
ings, plants, coins, and all sorts of curios, which in riper
years led to the founding at Berlin of a library, museum,
and model horticultural garden. Fond of bodily exercise, he early learned to ride, fence, fight, and snare
birds and rabbits. At twelve he shot his first deer,
and in later life became famous for his skill and endurance in hunting the wolves, bears, stags and wild
boars with which his lands abounded.

At fourteen, while the war continued to rage in Germany, Frederick William was sent to study in the stimulating atmosphere of Holland. He listened to lectures
at the University of Leyden, famous in physics and
mechanics. He delighted in visits to his Orange relatives, his maternal grandmother being a daughter of the
great William the Silent. Whether or not Frederick
William directly inherited characteristics from the famous Dutch statesman and general one cannot say; but
at any rate he resembled him in some of his noblest
qualities. At the camp of his great-uncle, Frederick
Henry of Orange, who was continuing the fight for
Dutch independence against the Spanish, he saw the
art of war developed by one of the ablest captains of
the age. In long letters to his father, describing the
campaigns and illustrating them with sketches, the
future victor of the battles of Warsaw and Fehrbellin
already gave evidence of keen interest and military in-
sight. At Frederick Henry's headquarters he also met
many of the leading statesmen of the day and learned
something of diplomacy. He talked with John Maurice
of Nassau, who had organized a colony in Brazil, and

was thrilled by the accounts of distant lands and riches overseas. But what most impressed his practical mind was the advanced agricultural methods of the Dutch, their wealth from ship-building and trade, their excellent canals, their art and architecture, and their generally high level of intelligence and culture. All these things remained lively memories, refreshed later by the employment of many Hollanders; they stirred ambitions which later ripened with rich advantage to his own more backward lands.

Frederick William also visited Cleves and made such a good impression on the Estates that they begged the Elector to appoint him Governor of Cleves. Frederick William eagerly supported their plea. But George William, more and more under the influence of Schwartzenberg, and fearing his son was becoming too independent, ordered him home. Frederick William was loath to leave the land where he had spent four such happy and profitable years. Delaying his departure on various pretexts for several months, he finally returned to Berlin in 1638. After dining with Schwartzenberg, he suddenly fell sick with a fever and rash. To his dying day he believed that Schwartzenberg, whose policies he hated and whom he believed to be responsible for his recall from Holland, had tried to poison him. Probably, however, he had only had an attack of measles. He spent the next two years at Königsberg in melancholy inactivity, because his father, at Schwartzenberg's advice, refused to initiate him into any government business, and thus deprived him of an opportunity of training for the duties which were soon to fall to him. Finally, on December 1, 1640, George William died of dropsy at forty-six, and "The New Master" took the reins.

END OF THE THIRTY YEARS' WAR, 1640-1648

How discouraging was the prospect which faced the youthful Elector! All his territories were more or less occupied by foreign forces. Swedish soldiers held the northern part of Brandenburg and were fighting to conquer the rest of it from the allied troops of Schwartzenberg and the Emperor. The Swedes were also firmly established in the whole of Pomerania, and the Emperor was inclined to let them keep it in disregard of Brandenburg's just claim to it. In Prussia the Swedish toll collectors had withdrawn, but their place had been taken by Poles. In Cleves-Mark many of the towns were in the hands of the Dutch, the Imperialists or the Hessians. Even more distressing to a prince who held absolutist views was the fact that in each of his territories the Elector's authority had vanished to a shadow before the selfish "privileges" of the local Estates. He had no available revenues and no dependable troops with which to assert his authority at home or abroad.

Furthermore, the ravages of war had wrought terrible ruin. Battle, murder, starvation and suicide had swept away more than half the population of Brandenburg. Fields went out of cultivation; roads and bridges were impassable; clipped and counterfeit coins drove out good money; and commerce decayed. Berlin, which had frequently ransomed itself from complete destruction by heavy payments had only 6000 inhabitants in 1640 compared with 14,000 in 1618, Frankfort on the Oder 2000 instead of 12,000, and Prenzlau on the Pomeranian frontier 600 instead of 9000! The open unfortified peasant villages suffered even more severely than the towns. Hundreds had been burned to the ground and become a wilderness for wolves, the peasants having been completely exterminated. The total number of the Great Elector's subjects at his accession had shrunk from about a million and a half before the war to hardly 600,000 souls: about 240,000 in Brandenburg (including the New Mark), 260,000 in Prussia, and 100,000 in Cleves, Mark and Ravensberg. Thus his total population in 1640 was no larger than that of a good-sized American city of today, such as Buffalo or Milwaukee. But by his death in 1688 he had much more than doubled it—to about 1,500,000— partly by acquiring new lands, partly by settling new colonists, and partly by the relatively great prosperity which he introduced.

Realizing his weakness from lack of money and dependable troops, Frederick William began his reign prudently by gently conciliating his enemies at home and abroad. Instead of dismissing the hated Schwartzenberg, as was generally expected, he left him as Governor of Brandenburg until the rioting of his own disorderly soldiery conveniently frightened him to death four months later. He reinstated at once, however, the Lutheran and Calvinist councilors whom Schwartzenberg had forced out of the Privy Council, and appointed some young and energetic friends of his own, like Conrad von Burgsdorf, and a little later Blumenthal, Waldeck and Schwerin. He adopted the wise practice which he later recommended to his son in his characteristic Advice of 1667:

In council give earnest attention. Note well the opinions of all the councilors, and also have a careful record kept. In matters which are important and where secrecy is necessary, make no final decision in the presence of the councilors, but take the question home to think over; after-

wards have one or another of the Privy Councilors and a
secretary come to you; think over again all the opinions
which were expressed, and make then your own decision.
Be like the bee, which sucks the sweetest juice from all
the flowers. If it is a difficult question, pray God that He
will enlighten your heart as to what you must do or leave
undone, in order that it may be for the honor of His name
and of your lands and peoples and subjects, and also to
the best advantage of yourself and your house.

To secure the good-will of his Polish overlord, the
young Elector journeyed to Warsaw, knelt before Ladis-
las IV, and was invested with the Duchy of Prussia.
He further promised to permit the construction of
Catholic churches, to pay an annual tribute, and to
exclude Calvinists from office in Prussia. Having thus
strengthened himself against Polish interference, he
returned to Königsberg and secured the homage of the
Prussian Estates by confirming their traditional privileges.

Meanwhile, Conrad von Burgsdorf had been des-
patched to Brandenburg to relieve the Electorate from
the double scourge of Schwartzenberg's soldiery and
the Swedish attacks. The troops which Schwartzenberg hired in alliance with the Emperor had, as he himself complained, mostly been "blown away like scum
on the sea." Though less than 5000 remained, he had
made a last effort to drive back the Swedes in order
to justify his pro-Austrian policy. It not only failed
completely, but stirred the Swedes to retaliate by ad-
vancing against Berlin. One of Schwartzenberg's last
and most hated acts was his burning some of the houses
outside the walls lest they afford a shelter for the
enemy's attack. The New Master in Königsberg, however, sent orders to stand strictly on the defensive as a

preliminary to negotiations for an armistice. Without sufficient troops to expel the Swedes, he believed it wiser to negotiate with them. This would also make it possible for him to reduce Schwartzenberg's disorderly soldiery, as he had been urgently begged to do by a delegation from the Brandenburg Estates. An armistice with the Swedes and a reduction of troops were to go hand-in-hand.

The remnants of Schwartzenberg's soldiery (*soldatesca*) represented the worst scum of Europe. As was customary in the Thirty Years' War, they had been recruited under the old regimental mercenary system, in which the colonel received a lump sum for raising and equipping a regiment, which he regarded as his own private property. Only when it was mustered for review by the prince who was paying for it would the colonel make frantic attempts to show a full regiment. Usually he did so only by resorting to devious frauds, such as making the same soldier pass in review several times, borrowing soldiers temporarily from brother colonels, or enrolling ruffians and hangers-on hastily gathered at the moment. Col. Klitzing, for example, who had received 40,000 talers from Schwartzenberg for supposedly 2200 soldiers, actually had on foot less than 100. A colonel, having pocketed his money, often defied the prince whom he had sworn to serve and plundered the people he was supposed to protect. He was as tyrannical over his ruffian soldiers as over the cowering civilian population. For small offenses he flogged them, branded them, sliced off their ears and noses, and compelled them to endure the torture of running the gauntlet. Several of these unruly colonels refused to obey orders from the new Elector. One of them, after browbeating the pastor and citizens of

Spandau, defiantly threatened to blow up the fortress and set fire to the town he was paid to defend. The population of Brandenburg complained bitterly that the soldier within the gates was far more terrible than the Swede without, and renewed their prayer to Frederick William that he disband the unruly *soldatesca*.

Conrad von Burgsdorf therefore proceeded energetically against Schwartzenberg's colonels. Some were arrested; others fled; a few loyal ones were retained and took a new oath to the Elector alone but not to the Emperor as heretofore. From the men in the ranks were dropped the undesirable and the unfit. From one regiment, for instance, Burgsdorf purged thirty-three native-born Swedes, thirty-two Scotch, Irish and Polish adventurers, and thirty men "crooked, lame and useless."

Those who were retained in service numbered less than 2500, merely enough to garrison the fortresses. But they formed a tiny nucleus for a new and relatively well-disciplined army. It was composed so far as possible of the Great Elector's own subjects, so that it might feel that it was fighting for the defense of home and country. It was sufficiently well paid so that it did not have to resort to the plunder and oppression of the people it was supposed to protect, and it was soon decently uniformed in blue. In the last years of the Thirty Years' War it was gradually increased to nearly 8000 men, partly supported by grants from the grateful Estates, and was a decisive factor in winning for Frederick William respectful consideration in the long negotiations leading to the Peace of Westphalia.

By excluding the Imperialists from Brandenburg, Frederick William succeeded in making an armistice with the Swedes in July, 1641. Swedish troops were to remain in occupation of six towns and were to be allowed peaceful passage through the Electorate, but otherwise Frederick William regained control of his Brandenburg lands and relieved them from further devastation. The armistice was for a term of two years, but was later extended until the final peace in 1648.

The armistice, however, did not include Pomerania, which remained completely in Swedish hands. To secure this and to establish sea-power on the Baltic, Frederick William secretly sought the hand of Queen Christina of Sweden. She, however, like Queen Elizabeth of England, had no intention of binding herself to a husband. So Frederick William finally abandoned this hope, and in 1646 sought an alliance with the Dutch by marrying Louise Henrietta, the daughter of Frederick Henry of Orange. Small in stature, tender and devoted, she proved an excellent wife until her death in 1667. The pleasant castle of Oranienburg, some thirty miles north of Berlin, named in her honor, became one of the favorite residences of the young couple.

At the long peace negotiations to end the Thirty Years' War, which took place from 1644 to 1648 at Münster and Osnabrück in Westphalia, Frederick William was not personally present. But through his delegates he strove energetically to secure primarily two things: legal recognition for his co-religionists, the Calvinists (or "Reformed" as they were generally called), and the possession of the whole of Pomerania.

In his first aim he was successful, in spite of the opposition of the Lutherans who set up an even more determined opposition than the Catholics. By the Treaty of Westphalia Calvinists were given the same

legal recognition in the Empire which Lutherans and
Catholics had enjoyed since the Peace of Augsburg of
1555. Largely through his influence there was added
also the tolerant provision that no prince should henceforth make use of his *jus reformandi,* i.e., his right of
compelling conformity by expelling subjects who differed in religion from himself.

In the Pomeranian question, however, he was less
successful. It was generally admitted that by earlier
treaties he had a just claim to the whole of Pomerania
after the death of the last duke in 1637. But the
Swedes were in occupation and claimed it as one of the
spoils of war; otherwise they would not make peace.
The Emperor and most of the German princes were inclined to let them keep it to get rid of them, even at
the sacrifice of the Elector's rights. But with the support of the French and the Dutch, Frederick William
finally secured a compromise. Pomerania was partitioned. The Swedes kept Western or Hither Pomerania, including the valuable port of Stettin, the mouth
of the Oder, and a strip of territory along its east bank.
Frederick William was given Eastern or Further Pomerania with the less good port of Colberg. To compensate him for the rest of his claim, he was also given
several secularized bishoprics: Cammin, adjoining Pomerania on the east; Minden on the Weser, serving as a
link toward the eventual connection of Brandenburg
and Ravensberg to the west; Halberstadt; and the
expectancy to the great Bishopric of Magdeburg (i.e.,
possession upon the death of the Saxon incumbent
which occurred in 1680). All these new lands, especially Halberstadt and Magdeburg which rounded out
the Electorate to the southeast, greatly strengthened
the growing importance of the Hohenzollerns. Next to

the Hapsburgs, they had become the strongest ruling
family in Germany.

THE NORTHERN WAR, 1655-1660

The Thirty Years' War was followed by seven years
of peace (1648-1655), but not of perfect calm. The
unexecuted clauses of the Treaty of Westphalia, the
continuance of war between France and Spain, a conflict between Brandenburg and Neuburg, and the increasing hostility between Sweden and Poland caused a
feeling of general insecurity which made the peace little
better than an armed truce. Nevertheless, Frederick
William was able to begin some of the remarkable
reforms which will be described in a later section. He
was unfortunately interrupted in this by the war
between Sweden and Poland.

In 1654 Queen Christina of Sweden wearied of shock-
ing Europe by reveling in masculine clothes and oaths
and by performing feats in horsemanship and hunting.
Giving Europe a new thrill, she suddenly abdicated
the throne of Gustavus Adolphus, abjured Lutheranism,
and lived for some thirty years, more picturesquely
than piously, as a Roman Catholic in the Eternal City.
The crown of Sweden fell to her warlike and ambitious
cousin, Charles. In one of his first council meetings he
urged that Sweden needed to make war as a means of
drawing out of the country the lazy and disorderly
soldiery who had returned from the Thirty Years' War
and had become a plague in the land. Passing in review the countries whom he might attack, Charles X
picked on Poland: his family had dynastic claims to
Poland, and the conquest of Poland would enable him
to carry out the Swedish dream of turning the Baltic

into a Swedish lake. In July, 1655, Swedish troops unceremoniously marched across the Great Elector's territory of Eastern Pomerania to attack Poland.

Faced with this danger of the Northern War upon his borders, without any considerable troops on hand of his own, and unable to count on effective co-operation from any of the European powers, Frederick William was in a perilous position. He was in danger of being engulfed in the war and of losing Prussia and Pomerania. He saw three courses open to him. (1) He might adopt neutrality, in spite of Machiavelli's dictum that it is folly for a prince to be neutral when his neighbors fall to fighting and so to run the risk of being later overwhelmed by the victor. (2) He might join the Swedes, and with their help hope to throw off the Polish overlordship over East Prussia and to conquer Polish West Prussia, thus consolidating Brandenburg, Eastern Pomerania and Prussia into a solid block of connected territory. (3) Or he might fight on the side of Poland, in accordance with his legal obligation as a vassal of the Polish king, and hope to conquer Swedish (Western) Pomerania which he failed to get at the Peace of Westphalia. His councilors were divided in opinion as between these alternatives. Frederick William therefore followed his own judgment. He adopted a skillful but unscrupulous opportunism, justified only, if at all, by the difficulties of his situation and the success with which he extricated himself. He proceeded to adopt one after another all three of the above alternative courses!

To command respect for his first policy, that of neutrality, Frederick William's prime need was a sizeable army. Aside from his modest military escort of 63 Horse Guards and 202 Life Guards, his Lilliputian army of 4000 was barely sufficient to garrison his widely scattered fortresses, let alone being utterly inadequate to defend the frontiers against fighting Poles and Swedes. He therefore had his officers begin at once to recruit a regular army in the Cleves and Brandenburg territories and called out the militia in East Prussia. By September, 1655, he had an army of 8000; by June, 1656, 18,000; and by the end of the war 27,000.

The Brandenburg Estates at first refused to grant any money for the support of these troops. They declared that Brandenburg was not in direct danger from the Poles or Swedes; that they were under no obligations to defend Frederick William's other lands; if East Prussia was in danger, let it look out for its own safety. To this parochial view the Elector replied with characteristic breadth of outlook, July 12, 1655: "The military preparations of all our neighbors compel us to follow their example. And since this army is for the benefit not simply of one, but of all my lands, I deem it proper that the cost and maintenance of the troops must be borne by all my lands, and that the soldiery must be assigned among them proportionally." When the Estates still refused, preferring "to trust in God and wait patiently upon events," Frederick William proceeded to the extreme step of collecting a land-tax of 180,000 talers by military execution. After this sign of his determination, the Estates "with much lamenting" granted considerable sums for the maintenance of the army during the Northern War.

Meanwhile Charles X had marched victoriously into Poland. The fickle Poles quickly recognized him as king, and their own ruler, John Casimir, fled the country. After a few months, however, the brutality of the Swedish soldiers and their desecration of Catholic churches and monasteries brought about a new revulsion of Polish feeling. A national Polish uprising against the invader and the return of John Casimir forced Charles X back to the frontier of Prussia. Wishing to avoid a conflict with the Brandenburg-Prussian troops, he was glad to enter into negotiations. So Frederick William turned from neutrality to alliance with Sweden. By the Treaty of Königsberg (Jan. 17, 1656) he established friendship with Charles X and recognized him, instead of John Casimir, as King of Poland and therefore as his overlord in East Prussia; and by the Treaty of Marienburg (June 25) he made a definite alliance, joined his army with that of the Swedes, and was promised in return a considerable slice of Poland when it should be conquered. To conquer this and to suppress the Polish national uprising Charles X and Frederick William then marched together toward the Polish capital. In the great three-day Battle of Warsaw (July 28-30) the allied force of 18,000 put to rout 70,000 undisciplined Polish troops. For the first time, soldiers from Brandenburg, Prussia and Cleves-Mark fought side by side under a single flag and a single leader for a single common purpose—the strengthening of the dynastic power of the Hohenzollern family. The new army, which strikingly embodied the new Brandenburg-Prussian State had borne gloriously its first baptism of fire.

The Battle of Warsaw, however, was more glorious than advantageous. *Minor victoriae fructus quam pro gloria fuit,* as Pufendorf shrewdly observed. The capture of the Polish capital did not mean the end of the war. Pestilence broke out in the allied armies and they were compelled to retreat into Prussia. Here Frederick William was able to force Charles X, as the price of his continuing the alliance, by the Treaty of Labiau (Nov. 26) to abandon the overlordship and recognize him as sovereign in Prussia. It now only remained for him to force John Casimir to do likewise.

The death of the Emperor, Ferdinand III, on April 2, 1657, his son's desire to secure the Brandenburg vote at the imperial election, and the skillful intrigues of the Hapsburg diplomatist, Lisola, paved the way for Frederick William's third political somersault. By the Treaty of Wehlau (Sept. 19, 1657), he allied with Poland against Sweden, and was promised that he should rule in full sovereignty (*jure supremi domini*) in East Prussia and receive the tiny Polish districts of Lauenburg, Bütow and Draheim on the Pomeranian frontier. A little later he allied with the Emperor also, with the aim of driving the Swedes out of Germany altogether. While his Catholic allies conquered part of Swedish Pomerania, Frederick William's army defeated the Swedish force which had occupied the Danish lands.

But as the Northern War became more general, France, England and the Dutch put pressure on the allies to make peace. The sudden death of Charles X afforded a favorable opportunity. By the general peace signed on May 3, 1660, at the monastery of Oliva, on the shore of the Baltic, north of Danzig, Frederick William finally won "his best jewel"—the prize that he had ever kept before his mind during the tortuous diplomacy of the Northern War—namely, the recognition by his neighbors of his sovereignty in Prussia. The humiliating Polish overlordship which had existed since 1466, as well as the temporary Swedish overlordship of 1656, was at an end. Since Prussia was not a part of the Holy Roman Empire, Frederick William had raised himself above his fellow German princes, who theoretically were under the Emperor; by the strength of his army and by his new position in Prussia he had elevated himself to the rank of a European sovereign. But would his own Prussian subjects recognize him as sovereign?

THE STRUGGLE FOR ABSOLUTISM

War almost inevitably leads to a great increase in the activity and power of the prince or the central government. Military efficiency necessitates increased taxes; and increased taxes mean new methods, new officials, and more centralized administrative institutions. So it happened that the Thirty Years' War, and especially the Northern War, aided the Great Elector in building up a more unified administration and in establishing his absolutism at the expense of the Estates, thus doing away with the paralyzing "dualism" caused by the concessions extorted by the nobles and towns from his predecessors.

During the Thirty Years' War Schwartzenberg had forcibly collected military taxes over the protest of the Estates and had set up a War Council (*Kriegsrat*) of his own which effectually usurped the place of the Privy Council. By so doing, as well as by his pro-Catholic policy, he had aroused the intense hatred of the nobles and towns. The Great Elector, on the other hand, began his reign by trying to conciliate his Brandenburg subjects. The War Council was abolished and the Privy Council was restored. The armistice with the Swedes made possible a reduction of the *soldatesca* and military taxes. His requests to the Estates to grant money to increase the tiny force of 4000 troops maintained after the Peace of Westphalia led to long hagglings, which resulted in a few small grants by the Estates and some further military collections by the Elector.

Finally, in 1653, in view of the threatening conditions all over Europe, the Brandenburg Estates were persuaded to make a grant of 530,000 talers, to be paid in six annual installments, 59 per cent being raised by the towns and the remaining 41 per cent by the nobles (i.e., from their peasants). The Estates of course expected that after the six-year grant was exhausted they would be called together again whenever the Elector needed more money. In 1659, however, the Northern War was still going on and Frederick William simply continued to collect the indispensable taxes without any further grant by the Estates. So the Diet of 1653 was the last which ever met in Brandenburg. Its only surviving vestige was a committee (formerly of fifty, and later of twelve, deputies) whose chief task was to manage the old financial machinery (*Kreditwerk*) which had been established to take care of Joachim II's debts and which existed until Hardenberg's financial reform in 1821.

More important than the elimination of the Diet as an obstacle to the Elector's absolutism was the shrewd and skillful manner in which he transformed certain officials representing the rival power of the Diet into loyal and devoted agents of his own absolutist authority. Long before the Thirty Years' War the Estates met not only in a General Diet for the whole Electorate, but also in local assemblies (*Kreistage*) in the twenty-odd districts or "circles" into which Brandenburg and the New Mark were divided. Here they nominated one or more Directors for each district (*Kreisdirectores*) to look after their corporate interests in general, and in particular to supervise the collection of the non-military taxes granted by the General Diet. These consisted mainly of the old land-tax (*Hufenschoss*) raised by the nobles from their peasants, and the beer-tax raised by the towns.

During the Thirty Years' War, when foreign troops were overrunning Brandenburg and when the Elector had to raise, feed, and quarter troops of his own, he began to appoint local agents to aid him and to protect as far as possible the rights and property of his subjects. These agents were variously known as War Commissars (*Kriegskommissare* or *Marschkommissare*) or as District Commissars (*Kreiskommissare*), there being one, or more often two, for each district. They received and supervised the money granted by the Estates for military purposes, or, if this was insufficient, levied money and provisions by military execution. They conducted troops on the march through their district, assigned them quarters, regulated the supply of food and fodder, and sought to restrain as far as possible "insolence" and plundering by the *soldatesca*. They exercised a kind of police power. Their task was not easy: they sometimes had to make provision out of their own pocket and one was cudgeled for his pains. No wonder they were often reluctant to accept appointment or asked to be released from office. Nevertheless, they helped save their districts from an otherwise more dreadful fate. In selecting them, frequently upon the nomination of the district nobles themselves, the Elector was often shrewd enough to appoint as War Commissars the very nobles who were already serving as elected District Directors. The point is often argued by Prussian historians whether the War Commissar represented the Prince or the Estates. The fact is he represented both. He was an appointee of the Elector and was a prime factor in building up the Standing Army, which came to be the symbol of unity and strength in the Hohenzollern state. At the same time he had at heart the interests of his district and brother nobles, was usually a man of their choice (if he happened to be a Kreisdirector), and received a small compensation paid by them. In the second half of the seventeenth century he came to exercise increased police and judicial powers, acquired social prestige, and after 1702 rejoiced in the title of Rural Magistrate (*Landrat*). This officer, introduced from Brandenburg into the other Hohenzollern lands, remained ever after the chief local administrative officer in the rural districts, an invaluable agent of the central government, and a loyal and devoted servant of the Hohenzollern dynasty.

The *new* land-tax (*Kontribution*), granted for military purposes by the Estates during and immediately after the Thirty Years' War, but collected by the Elector after 1659 without any grant, was supervised by the War Commissars. As the private demesne lands of the nobles were exempt from this, and as he had had to haggle with the Estates to get it granted at all, the Great Elector had intended to supplement or replace it with a general assessment (*Assise* or *Akzise*) on consumption goods. This recently invented tax had proved a financial gold mine in France and Holland, as he had observed. Being an indirect tax and not demandable on any fixed date, its collection would be less noticed and opposed. It had the further advantage that the nobles would have to pay it, though of course the burden on them would be relatively much less than on the poorer classes. Just because it threatened their "privilege" of tax-exemption, the nobles successfully thwarted its general adoption. The Brandenburg towns, however, soon came to find it a very convenient way of raising their quota (59 per cent) of the military tax and began to adopt it. At first it was collected by the town magistrates; after 1682 it became an obligatory state tax collected in the towns by War-tax Commissars (*Steuerkommissare*) appointed by the Elector. These officials of the central government gradually took over the whole town administration in the name of the Elector, thus depriving the towns of the oligarchic self-government and political power which they had enjoyed since the Middle Ages. As a result of these financial innovations, the Brandenburg Estates, both the nobility and the towns, were eliminated as a check on the power of the prince. The Elector, on the other hand, had developed three important instruments of absolutism: an enlarged army, new taxes to support it, and new officials to carry the authority of the central government into the rural districts and urban centers.

In Cleves Mark the Estates resisted the Elector more successfully than in Brandenburg. Far removed from the center in Berlin, they got the backing of the Netherlands and of the Duke of Neuburg in Jülich so long as the Elector's authority remained provisional, i.e., until his treaty with Neuburg in 1666. The "privileges" on which they insisted were numerous: annual meetings without any summons or interference by the Elector; an oath of loyalty to their laws instead of to the Elector by all officials; no taxes, nor recruiting and garrisoning of troops, nor building of defense fortresses, nor even bringing in Electoral troops, except by consent of the Estates; and especially the "right of the native born" (*Indigenatsrecht*), by which the Elector could appoint no official in Cleves-Mark except a person who happened to be so fortunate as to have been born and to own property in the territories.

In spite of these pretensions, Frederick William managed to recruit some 6000 troops in Cleves-Mark during the Northern War. After the war, and especially after 1666, with the promise of Dutch subsidies to prevent the French conquest of the lower Rhine, with his standing army, and with his triumph over opposition in Brandenburg, he was able to take a firmer stand. He sent troops into Cleves-Mark and garrisoned them there, and curtailed some of the other privileges. The Estates still retained their right to meet and grant taxes, but soon recognized the Standing Army as a permanent institution, and made regular and even generous grants for its support, ranging from 110,000 talers in 1661 to 190,000 in 1687. In return the Elector respected the "right of the native born." At the time of his death in 1688 a very satisfactory harmony was established, and Cleves-Mark gradually became organically united with Brandenburg by accepting most of the Elector's centralizing institutions.

THE STRUGGLE FOR ABSOLUTISM IN PRUSSIA

In East Prussia the conflict with the Estates was more determined and bitter, owing to the peculiar bonds between Prussia and Poland and to the tragic opposition of Roth and Kalckstein. During more than two centuries the Prussian Estates had gradually acquired enormously wide "privileges," largely as a result of their habit of appealing to Poland against their own ruler—first against the Grandmaster and after 1525 against the Hohenzollern Dukes of Prussia. The "liberties" of which they boasted came to resemble the unbridled license of the Polish nobility, while the ducal power was whittled down almost to the vanishing point, as in the case of the politically impotent Polish kings of the seventeenth century. Many Prussian nobles held office or land in Poland, and could play a double rôle as Poles in Warsaw, and as Germans in Prussia. All Prussian subjects enjoyed since 1466 the right to carry cases on appeal from the Prussian courts to the courts of the Polish overlord. The Prussian Estates wanted to preserve the close bonds with Poland because they were the bulwark of their "liberties"; for the same reason the Great Elector wished to sever them. His request that the Estates recognize him as sovereign brought to a head a fundamental issue: medieval Polish feudalism or modern Hohenzollern absolutism; selfish local class privileges or the common good of the whole State.

At his accession in 1640, with the Thirty Years' War on his hands, the Great Elector had prudently confirmed the privileges of the Estates and so avoided raising the issue. During the Northern War, to be sure, he had been forced to levy a general excise tax and to recruit troops, and the Estates had accepted the exigencies of the situation, though not without protests. In 1660, however, with his sovereignty recognized in the Treaty of Oliva, and with his continued taxation and maintenance of troops, the issue became unavoidable. The Estates claimed that they were not bound by treaties in which they had not been consulted and to which they were not a party. They maintained that treaties affecting Prussia required the free consent of all three political factors: the King of Poland, the Duke of Prussia, and the Prussian Estates; that Prussia and

Poland formed a *corpus individuum, quod non separari potest;* and that this *nexus in aeternum* could not be dissolved by two of the parties without the consent of the third. They demanded therefore that the question be laid before a Polish Diet which should be attended by a deputation of the Prussian Estates, and that thus, in the presence of Estates, Elector, and King, new constitutional relations should be agreed upon and adopted.

Unable to come at once in person to Prussia, Frederick William sent his closest friend and wisest counselor, the gentle but firm Otto von Schwerin, to deal with the situation. He found a hostile and treacherous ferment on all sides. The nobles and towns demanded that he call a meeting of the Estates, redress their grievances in connection with the taxes and troops levied during the Northern War, and confirm all their ancient privileges.

The leading spirits among the nobles were Albert von Kalckstein and his son, Christian Ludwig. The father had enriched himself in Saxon military service during the Thirty Years' War and acquired considerable property in Prussia and Lusatia. In 1657 he had taken part in a conspiracy with Poland against the Elector's authority in Prussia. After the Treaty of Oliva he secretly joined with others in sending a letter urging Polish troops to re-occupy Prussia. His unfortunate son, Christian Ludwig von Kalckstein, had served in the French army under Turenne until dismissed as a disorderly character. He entered the Polish army in 1654, but in the Northern War raised a regiment for the Great Elector, fought on his side at the Battle of Warsaw, and was rewarded by the gift of the lucrative captaincy of the Prussian district of Oletzko. In 1659,

however, he was accused by the clerk of the district of
graft and maltreatment of the inhabitants, and was
consequently suspended from his captaincy by order of
the Elector. Thenceforth he was filled with the bitterest hatred. He re-entered the Polish army, and in 1661
was in Warsaw furthering his father's efforts to persuade the Poles to prevent Frederick William from
establishing his sovereignty in Prussia.

Hieronymus Roth was of more estimable personal
character, though more determined in his opposition to
the Elector's sovereignty. As a member of the powerful Merchants' Gild in Königsberg and a leading town
magistrate with the arts and convictions of a dema-
gogue, he incited opposition in the towns. He kept in
touch with Poland through his brother, a Jesuit in Warsaw, as well as by occasional visits by himself or his
son to Polish magnates.

In May, 1661, Schwerin summoned the Estates—the
"Great Diet"—which sat with interruptions from 1661
to 1663. Its debates and proceedings fill three large
volumes. Schwerin made a conciliatory proposal to
confirm most of the privileges in return for recognition
of the Elector's sovereignty. The proposal was at once
rejected. In addition to demands similar to those of
the Brandenburg and Cleves Estates—regular meetings, no taxes or troops or fortifications except by their
consent, the "right of the native born," and oppressive
control over the peasantry—the Prussian Diet insisted
on protection from competition of French, Scotch and
other foreign traders, exclusion from office of all Calvinists, continuance of the right of appeal to Polish
courts, and non-recognition of the Elector's sovereignty
except by a new agreement with Poland in which they
should participate.

Early in the session Schwerin perceived that Roth was the chief instigator of the opposition. He therefore invited him to the Castle for a private talk. Both men apparently lost their temper. According to Schwerin's account, Roth denounced the Elector as a tyrant and declared that never should he have the sovereignty, so that Schwerin doubted "whether the fellow was *sanae mentis* or filled with brandy." According to his own account, Roth merely quoted a noble who had called the Elector a tyrant, and had only said that he did not know what good the sovereignty would do him if the Estates retained all their privileges.

The conflict with the Estates dragged on for a year and seemed to approach a deadlock. The Lutheran clergy preached against the threatened "slavery"; the building of a Calvinist church in Königsberg was prevented by force; and there was the danger that Poland might actively intervene. Schwerin decided that Roth, as the chief fomenter of trouble, should be arrested. But this was not so easy, as Roth was protected by the people and Schwerin did not have sufficient troops to make it safe to attempt to seize him by force. Moreover, in March, 1662, surmising an effort to arrest him, Roth disguised himself as a monk and escaped to talk with the King of Poland. When he slipped back again to Königsberg, eluding the cavalry detachment on watch to pick him up, he kept in hiding. In June his son traveled secretly to Warsaw and urged John Casimir "no longer to permit that we should be excruciated in infamous and miserable ways." The King, who wanted to support the Prussians but did not want to risk another war with the Great Elector, gave young Roth a cautiously worded letter. The elder Roth interpreted this as a promise of support. Accordingly, he collected his followers in the Cathedral, read them John Casimir's letter, and invited them to swear to a "Pledge against the Foreign Councilors," i.e., against Schwerin. However, the oath was not taken on the spot, as the pledge was given over to the gilds to consider.

In this situation Frederick William decided to come in person to Königsberg, bringing with him some two thousand troops which were placed in strategic positions. He was highly indignant against Roth because of his sayings and doings as reported by Schwerin, and agreed that he ought to be arrested if it could be done without bloodshed. A ruse was successful. A small squad of soldiers was marched past the house where Roth was hiding; he put his head out of the window to see what was going on, was recognized, quickly seized, and carried to the Castle. Here he was brought to trial before a special commission composed of Prussian nobles and burghers. They found him guilty on five counts, but rejected the death penalty and urged a pardon. Even Schwerin advised his master that it would be wiser to win his subjects by clemency than to frighten them by an example of severity. The Elector, however, believing that Roth had insulted his person by calling him a tyrant and had incited the people against his authority, condemned him to imprisonment for life. On several occasions he intimated that if Roth would acknowledge his error and beg for a pardon it would be granted. Roth, equally determined and obstinate, refused, believing that in opposing the Elector's sovereignty he had constitutional right on his side. So he remained in mild captivity in the fortress of Peitz until his death in 1678. At the news of Roth's arrest,

Albert von Kalckstein, fearing a similar fate, hastily fled.

The Estates, deprived of their chief leaders, impressed by Frederick William's determined attitude, and coaxed by his conciliatory offers, finally yielded in May, 1663. They agreed to do homage to him as sovereign, provided Polish deputies were present as a matter of form to release them from their allegiance to Poland. He in return confirmed all their privileges so far as these did not conflict with his sovereign rights. He promised to call a Diet at least every six years; reduced somewhat the taxes and troops; and agreed that the Calvinists should not have more than four churches in Prussia and should only be admitted to a few minor offices. In gaining the essential point of sovereignty, Frederick William had won a triumph for himself personally and for the future of his state.

In 1669 the Estates again refused for months to grant taxes as requested. This renewed opposition contributed to seal the fate of Christian Ludwig von Kalckstein. After his father's death in 1667, he quarreled bitterly with his brother and sisters over the division of the elder Kalckstein's property. In their hatred they denounced him as having boasted of a threat to murder the Elector. At an examination before magistrates he was asserted to have boasted in public that he had planned a Polish invasion of Prussia in which he would burn and plunder; that in revenge for his suspension from the captaincy of Oletzko he would write "Suspended!" on the walls of the ruined Prussian towns; that if he came across the Elector and princes he would spare none but hew down all. So much of the evidence brought against him by his own relatives seemed inspired by family hatred rather than zeal for truth and justice, that the court was in doubt until Kalckstein conceived the unhappy idea of bribing two of his servants to take false names and give perjured testimony. This was discovered and made the court doubt the veracity of his denials of the allegations brought by his relatives. Accordingly, he was sentenced to life imprisonment.

When the Elector came to Königsberg six months later, Kalckstein humbly begged for mercy, and the sentence was generously changed from imprisonment for life to the payment of a fine. Instead of paying this he packed his money and valuables on sledges and fled on a winter's night to Warsaw. Here he turned Roman Catholic to curry favor with the Poles, and distributed handbills telling how the Great Elector was maltreating his subjects. All this was too much for Frederick William's patience. When the King of Poland refused to extradite Kalckstein, the Prussian agent in Warsaw managed to kidnap him, roll him in a rug, and hustle him across the frontier back into Prussia. Here in 1671 he was brought to trial a second time, even tortured to make him reveal the accomplices among the Prussian nobility at whom he had hinted, and finally condemned and executed for treason.

After this example of severity the Great Elector met very little further resistance from the Prussian Estates. From 1680 onwards he drew a regular military revenue from Prussia, consisting of a land-tax in the rural districts and small towns, and an excise tax in Königsberg, a financial separation as in Brandenburg which gave a deathblow to the corporate solidarity of the Estates and contributed to their final disappearance in 1705—except when called to do homage at the accession of a new sovereign.

SHIFTING ALLIANCES, 1660-1688

Never, except perhaps among the Italians of Machiavelli's day, were alliances so rapidly made and so ruthlessly broken as in the second half of the seventeenth century. In the diplomatic period following the Thirty Years' War religious interests had begun to lose their influence, and the political interest of the State (*Staatsräson*) was becoming increasingly the new and higher guiding rule of conduct of the absolutist princes. No prince was cleverer or more opportunist in this than the Great Elector, partly because of his shrewd practical common sense and determined character, and partly because his lands, scattered from the Meuse to the Memel, touched so many states that his diplomatic position was extremely complicated and precarious.

No brief narrative can give any adequate account of his numerous shifting alliances. Suffice it to say that, from the end of the Northern War to his death in 1688, Frederick William was several times in alliance with England, Holland, France, Denmark, Sweden, Austria, Spain and various German states, and often allied with several at the same time. Except for brief periods in 1668, 1670, 1673-4 and from 1679-86, when he was disgusted with his Dutch and Hapsburg allies and influenced by the hope of generous French subsidies to support his army, his broad Calvinism (and also the promise of Dutch subsidies) tended toward alliances with Holland and England to protect the Lower Rhine from the aggression of Louis XIV. As a patriotic German Prince receiving subsidies from the Empire, he was often in alliance with the Hapsburgs in defense of the Holy Roman Empire against the French and the

Turks. The kernel of his thought is to be found in the very interesting secret "Advice" to his son in 1667:

Alliances, to be sure, are good; but a force of one's own, on which one can rely, is better. A ruler is treated with no consideration if he does not have troops and means of his own. It is these, Thank God! which have made me *considerabel* since the time that I began to have them.

The Great Elector's alliances were mainly defensive but were also partly motivated by the fact that his lands were still too poor to support from his own resources an army large enough to defend his scattered territories and to enable him to follow a wholly independent foreign policy. His alliances therefore were often partly dictated by the hope of subsidies. From 1674 to 1688 these foreign subsidies totaled roughly 2,712,000 talers: 57,000 from Denmark, 467,000 from Spain, 503,000 from France, 912,000 from the Netherlands, and 973,000 from the Empire. As he was able during these years to squeeze only the equivalent of 20,000,000 for military purposes from his own lands, much of which was in the form of deliveries in kind instead of cash, and as he wisely refrained from borrowing heavily (less than 700,000 talers), these cash subsidies represented an important item in building up the army which was to make him "considerable."

War was forced upon the Great Elector a third time by Louis XIV's invasion of Holland in 1672. By treaty the Elector was to aid the Dutch, but he unfortunately sought to do so by marching with a Hapsburg force under Montecuccoli to the Middle instead of the Lower Rhine. The Elector was eager to push forward and divert Turenne from the Dutch, but Montecuccoli refused to cross the Rhine. So the Dutch withheld the promised subsidies, and the Elector, constantly held back by the balky Hapsburg horse to which he was yoked, withdrew for a year from the war. In 1674, with Turenne's invasion of the Palatinate and a declaration of war against the French by the Imperial Reichstag, Frederick William again took his place beside the Hapsburg army in defense of the Holy Roman Empire. The Allies drove the French back into Alsace and had a good chance to crush Turenne near Colmar, when the Elector's fiery zeal was again balked by the timidity and retreat of Montecuccoli's successor, Bournonville.

Meanwhile Louis XIV had bribed the Swedes with French gold to make a diversion in his favor by a Swedish invasion of Brandenburg. Gathering his troops together, Frederick William suddenly dashed back to the Elbe to protect his people. Pushing forward his cavalry under the Prince von Homburg, he caught the surprised Swedes on June 28, 1675, at Fehrbellin and won a decisive victory with some 6000 men against 8000. It was after this that he was hailed as the "Great" Elector, and the victory was later celebrated (with much poetic license) in Kleist's stirring drama, *Der Prinz von Homburg*. After Fehrbellin the Great Elector easily cleared the Swedes out of Brandenburg. In the course of the next three years he successfully besieged and stormed the fortresses of Stettin, Stralsund and Greifswald and conquered Swedish Pomerania.

In the winter of 1678-9 Louis XIV encouraged the Swedes to ship an army of 16,000 across the Baltic to invade Prussia from the northeast, but the Great Elector annihilated it by despatching a force which was marched or transported in sledges over the frozen lagoons of the Kurischer and Frischer Haff. By these victories he hoped at last to realize his claim to the whole of Pomerania, which he had not been able to make good at the Peace of Westphalia. He was doomed, however, to the bitterest disappointment. While he had been fighting the Swedish-French alliance on the shores of the Baltic, his allies had tired of the fight on the Rhine and signed the Treaty of Nymwegen giving to France Franche Comté and other territories belonging to the Holy Roman Empire. Louis XIV, who had occupied Cleves, was then in a position to use his great power to demand that Western Pomerania should be restored to Sweden.

Deserted by all his allies, and faced with a French threat to keep Cleves, Frederick William was forced to accept on June 29, 1679, just four years after his brilliant victory of Fehrbellin, the Peace of St. Germain: he regained possession of Cleves, but he had to give back to Sweden all his hard-won conquests in Swedish Pomerania except a little strip of land on the right bank of the Oder opposite Stettin. His indignation turned against the Hapsburgs and the Dutch who had left him in the lurch, rather than against the French who sought to soften his disappointment over Pomerania by giving him some compensation in cash. During the next six years, therefore, he allied with the French and received their subsidies. Only when Louis's seizure of Strasbourg foreshadowed further aggressions against Germany, and when his persecution of the Calvinists reached a climax in the Revocation of the Edict of Nantes in 1685, did the Great Elector return to his normal policy of defending the Empire and the Anglo-Dutch Protestant cause against the Catholic Monarch of Versailles. The last pass-word that he issued for the Guard at Potsdam the day before his death on

May 9, 1688, was significant: "Amsterdam and London!"

MILITARY REVENUES AND ADMINISTRATION

During the Northern War the Great Elector had raised his army from 4000 to an efficient force of 27,000, not including 4000 men serving in garrisons. After 1660 he decided upon the policy of maintaining in time of peace, as a *standing army,* about half the force which he had raised by necessity in time of war, as a fighting army. With characteristic thrift he found means of turning his standing army to profitable uses. Soldiers were employed in digging the famous Frederick William Canal connecting the Elbe and the Oder, thus making Berlin the center of water transportation between Central Europe and Hamburg. Soldiers were conveniently used in transforming the Tiergarten into a pleasant park and suburb and connecting it with Berlin by a broad avenue planted with linden trees which became celebrated among travelers as "Unter den Linden." In the war with France and Sweden the army was again increased to a fighting force of 45,000 in 1678, but with the return of peace, as in 1660, was again reduced by somewhat more than one-half, making a "considerable" standing army of about 18,000. This remained its average size until Louis XIV's invasion of the Palatinate in 1686, when it was increased again to 30,000. It made Brandenburg-Prussia, next to Austria, the strongest power in Germany and a highly prized ally in later wars.

The indirect effects of the standing army on internal administration were perhaps even more important than its direct effects on foreign policy in self-defense and new conquests. As the army was one of the first institutions which embodied the unity and efficiency of the whole Brandenburg-Prussian State, in contrast with the weakness and corner-grocery attitude of the separate territories, so the organs of financial administration which were developed for the army's support soon came to form a centralized and efficient civil service. This gradually supplanted the various lax and decentralized agencies which had been managed by the Estates. By the time of the Great Elector's death, his absolutist officials had pretty generally taken the place of the particularistic agents of the Estates. So the two main pillars of the Prussian State arose side by side: the standing army and the civil service. This is a complicated subject, but a simplified statement of it, with the aid of the table at the end of the volume, will make clear its more important features, and will also indicate how local Brandenburg institutions (shown by dotted lines in the table) were extended to the Elector's other lands and were thus transformed into general organs (shown by solid lines) of the whole Brandenburg-Prussian State (*Gesammtstaat*).

Until the Northern War the troops in the Elector's various lands had stood under separate commands and never been united in a single army. As a first step toward centralization Freiherr von Sparr was given authority in 1651 over all the garrison troops except those in Brandenburg and Prussia; then in 1655 he was given general command over *all* the troops. If the Great Elector took over personally the command, as at the Battle of Warsaw and on many other campaigns, Sparr acted as his Chief of Staff. By the time of his death in 1668 Sparr had formed a group of officers into a permanent General Staff (*Generalstab*).

Under Sparr's formal authority, but virtually independent of him, was the far more important General Commissariat. This was an extension of the system of War Commissars who had received and dispensed the new military tax (*Kontribution*) collected during the Thirty Years' War as already noted. In the Electorate and in each of the other territories a single Chief Commissar (*Oberkriegskommissar*) had been given authority over the District Commissars. In 1655 General Platen, a very able man who spoke several languages and had been on many missions, as well as having served as District Commissar in Priegnitz and as Privy Councilor since 1651, was appointed General Commissar for the whole State. He and his successors built up a well-organized General Commissariat (*Generalkommissariat*) for overseeing the collection and dispensing of the *Kontribution* from *all* the Great Elector's lands. The collection of this tax had at first been in the hands of the agents of the Estates, but as their power was undermined, the collection was taken over, in most of the territories by 1688, by the General Commissar's subordinates: the Chief Commissar in each province and by their sub-officials, the District Commissars (*Kreiskommissare* in the rural districts, *Steuerkommissare* in the towns and *Aemterkommissare* on the Elector's domain lands).

The General Commissariat also saw to the recruiting, provisioning and quartering of the army. It looked after the military hospitals, the care of invalid soldiers, and the exercise of military justice. Like a modern war department, it had charge of everything relating to the army except questions of strategy and leadership in the field which belonged to the General Staff. Its most important function, however, was to increase the military revenue and find other fruitful sources besides the *Kontribution*. It devised the productive graduated poll-taxes of 1677-9 during the Swedish-French War, in which the 250 gradations, covering every individual from "Our most gracious Master" at 1000 talers to postilions, poor artisans and peasants at one taler each, read like a fascinating social register. It budded off a number of boards which were to tap or create taxable wealth: a *Commerzcollegium* to stimulate commerce and afford merchants speedy justice; a Stamp-tax Chest (*Stempelkasse*) to collect the revenue from the sale of the specially stamped paper required for legal documents; a so-called French Commissariat to bring in and settle the industrially valuable Huguenot refugees; and a Navy Chest (*Marinekasse* or *Chargenkasse*) to collect a tax from all public officials (with the kindly exception of clergy and school teachers) of one-half the first year's salary —a tax similar to the ecclesiastical "first fruits"— used originally toward creating a tiny navy but soon applied to the army. In its management of the grain stores and its other economic, political, and police activities the General Commissariat was a powerful factor in introducing mercantilism and prosperity by compulsion.

In 1652 the military correspondence, which had hitherto been handled for the Privy Council by the Elector's Privy Chancery, was delegated to a War Secretary under whom there developed in 1657 a Privy War Chancery (*Geheime Kriegskanzlei*). This issued the commissions for newly appointed officers, carried on the military correspondence, and kept the general records relating to the army. It worked in two rooms over the kitchen in the Berlin Schloss for a century— until in 1745 its paper records, unfortunately for the historian, were used by Frederick the Great to make wadding for cartridges! Besides this body, Sparr and Platen also had for their respective organizations special chanceries (*Feldmarschallskanzlei* and *Kommissariatskanzlei*).

After Schwartzenberg's military fiasco, the keeping and accounting of the meager Brandenburg military revenues, consisting mainly of the *Kontribution,* the bushel-tax on grain, and certain war-tolls, was done by their respective treasuries or chests (*Kontributionskasse, Metzkasse,* and *Lizentenkasse*), which in 1651 were merged into the War Chest (*Kriegskasse*). This continued till the end of the century primarily as a provincial Brandenburg receptacle, though it also received some revenues from the other provinces and was to that extent a general or central institution. During the Northern War, in order to provide cash on the spot for the needs of the marching army, there was created a Field War Chest (*Feldkriegskasse*). This sucked money from all the provinces, and after 1674 was enriched by the foreign subsidies and kept an invaluable account book which has been preserved.

CIVIL REVENUES AND ADMINISTRATION

In seventeenth century Brandenburg, unlike modern states, civil and military revenues were wholly different and distinct from one another. The latter, though of more recent origin, were soon larger in amount and more important in the proliferation of centralizing institutions in the growing absolutist State. The civil revenues, to use a modern term, or, more properly, the patrimonial income of the prince, originated in the Middle Ages and in the Great Elector's day were still of a primitive and semi-feudal character. They were chiefly of two sorts: (1) the domain revenues managed by the Comptroller's Office (*Amtskammer*) and consisting of money rents and of "payments in kind," such as grain, cattle, dairy produce, and fire-wood, from the surplus product of the manorial lands which the Electors kept and had cultivated for their own needs; and (2) the "regalian rights," consisting of the profits of justice like fines, tolls on roads and rivers and harbors, a beer-tax, a tax on Jews, and profits from coinage and from various commercial monopolies like the salt, postal, glass, iron, copper, and millstone administrations. The regalian revenues were paid partly into the Exchequer (*Hofrentei*) and partly into the Privy Purse (*Chatulle*).

All the civil revenues were frightfully depleted by the terrible ravages and general economic desolation of the Thirty Years' War. In Brandenburg more than half of the population and cattle had disappeared and nearly half of the tillable land had become "waste." In the administration of the Elector's domain lands the stewards kept no proper accounts and often kept for themselves what they should have turned in at Berlin. As about five-sixths of the domain revenues were in the form of natural products which were not evaluated in cash equivalents, and as all officials received the greater part of their salaries from these natural products instead of in cash, no one had any notion of the total amount and value of the domain revenues or cost of the Elector's Household and administration. Many of the domains had been mortgaged during the long war and so either produced nothing or were a positive burden. Even those which the Electors had managed to retain were burdened by their convenient but careless habit of making gifts or payments by "assignments" upon this or that domain revenue—sometimes when no such revenue actually existed; worse still, no accounting was made of these prodigal assignments.

The Great Elector, well aware of the financial evils, sought to remedy them soon after the war was over. In 1651 he appointed a commission of four of his ablest advisors with the significant new title of State Treasury Councilors (*Staatskammerräte*) to reform the management of the domains in all his lands. Unfortunately, they were so occupied with their other duties as active Privy Councilors and other matters, and then with the Northern War, that they accomplished virtually nothing. Nor did the individual men (Canstein, Grumbkow, Jena, Gladebeck and Meinders) who followed them from 1659 to 1683 do much better, except that in 1673 there was established a Court State Chest (*Hofstaatskasse*). This new treasury (making three, with the *Chatulle* and *Hofrentei*) was created to assure a larger and more regular income for the Elector's expanding Household and State administration. It was therefore provided with a certain fairly fixed income from various domains and from the local exchequers of *all* the Elector's lands. Until 1674 some of these revenues from Prussia, Cleves and elsewhere had been paid into the two Brandenburg treasuries, the *Chatulle* and *Hofrentei*, which to a certain extent had therefore been *general* treasuries for the Brandenburg-Prussian State. After the establishment of the *Hofstaatskasse*, however, the *Hofrentei* sank back again into a provincial Brandenburg exchequer and therefore came to be known as a *Landrentei*.

In 1683 an East Frisian Baron, Dodo zu Knyphausen, whose great ability was equaled by his great modesty, entered Frederick William's service. He at last accomplished revolutionary reforms in the administration of the domains and greatly increased the revenues from them. He gradually redeemed the manorial estates which had been mortgaged. He let out the domains on short leases (*Arrende* or *Püchte*) so that he was sure of fixed rents instead of trusting to the doubtful honesty of managing stewards. He translated all "payments in kind" into cash equivalents. He required strict quarterly accountings of all "assignments" as well as of all domain cash-rents and produce and of all Household and other administrative payments. He was thus able in 1689 to draw up for the first time a decent budget (*General État*) of all the Elector's civil revenues and expenditures from all his lands. It showed a handsome civil cash revenue of 1,533,000 talers, as compared with a meager 297,000 in 1664 and a pitiful 59,000 in 1644. Knyphausen also organized, to assist him, a board (*collegium*) of technical experts known in 1689 as the Privy Comptroller's Office (*Geheime Hofkammer*).

PROSPERITY BY COMPULSION

Besides developing these various means for extracting larger military and civil revenues, the Great Elector took innumerable measures for increasing the population, prosperity and productivity of his lands, thus lessening the financial burden upon the individual.

In 1649 he settled seventy Frisian families, well acquainted with the better agricultural methods of the Dutch, in Brandenburg. A generation later he brought in eighty Swiss families. With characteristic toleration he admitted Jews from Poland who paid annual tribute money for protection against prevailing hatred and prejudice and who 'had to promise not to charge usurious rates of interest or deal in stolen goods. Most valuable were the 20,000 refugee French Huguenots whom Frederick William aided to settle by sending them guides and traveling money and by giving them land, building material, exemption from taxes for six years, and many other privileges. They formed at one time a sixth of the population of Berlin with a church and a school conducted in French, and helped immeasurably to raise its economic and cultural level by their new industries and quick intelligence. They enriched the Electoral dinner table by popularizing the eating of lettuce, asparagus, cauliflowers and artichokes. From their numbers were formed a cavalry regiment under Baron Briquemault and an infantry regiment under the Marquis de Varenne. Two companies of young French nobles, the *Grands Mousquetaires*, gorgeous in red coats, gold braid and white-feathered hats, served as a kind of officers' training school from whose descendants came many distinguished Prussian officers.

For a century and a half the Counts of Thurn and Taxis had enjoyed an imperial monopoly for their postal system throughout Germany, with many offices in foreign cities. To take its place in his own lands and save its charges, the Great Elector established in 1662 a postal system of his own. It carried at first only official despatches, then letters and packages for others, and finally coach passengers. With Berlin as the center of the postal network, it aided the process of centralization of government by putting the central boards in quick touch with the local ones. The post went twice a week from Königsberg through Berlin to Cleves in what was considered in those days as the incredibly quick time of one week. The postal system, like the

Prussian State Railways of two centuries later of which it was the fore-runner, was also agreeably remunerative, its profits showing a uniformly upward curve from 17,000 talers in 1662 to 80,000 in 1688.

The purchase and sale of salt from Lüneburg or Hamburg was also exploited by the Great Elector as a profitable government monopoly (without the abuses of the French *gabelle*), and averaged a return of more than 40,000 talers a year from 1662 to 1680. After 1680, when the acquisition of the Magdeburg lands gave him possession of a salt supply of his own (the Stassfurt and Halle deposits which are among the richest salt-beds in Europe), the salt monopoly became much more productive until it was finally abolished in 1867. The millstone monopoly brought in a small but steady revenue, but the efforts for the state exploitation of iron, copper, glass and some other manufactures were financial failures.

For the promotion of agriculture the Great Elector ran a botanical garden and experimental station in front of the Berlin Palace for trying out foreign trees and plants of all sorts as to suitability for his sandy lands. The Oranienburg estate, named after his first wife, where Dutch methods were employed, was also a model farm for all his subjects. To promote the planting of fruit-trees he decreed that no bridegroom on his domains might marry until he had first planted at least six new trees.

By the application of his native common sense and by the trial-and-error method, rather than by mere copying of Dutch and French mercantilist notions, Frederick William rigorously supervised the gilds and controlled exports and imports after the mercantilist fashion in the interests of his people as a whole. In his efforts to create a navy and found colonies, however, he was two centuries ahead of his time; he and his successors soon found that their resources were still too small to compete successfully with the ruthless colonial and naval power of the Dutch, the French and the English. So his successors wisely confined their main efforts to strengthening their power on the continent of Europe.

CHAPTER III

THE DEVELOPMENT OF THE PRUSSIAN STATE, 1688-1786

IT was a curious trait of the Hohenzollern dynasty that the heir was usually a contrast to the ruling prince. This often caused unedifying family discord, for the father could not understand the son, and the son could not appreciate the good qualities of the father. For the Prussian State, however, this family trait was not wholly unfortunate, but rather the reverse, for the son supplied qualities which were lacking in the father but which were valuable for the State. The Great Elector's son, Frederick (1688-1713), lacked the solid financial understanding and practical administrative sense of the Great Elector, but his passion for pomp and dignity and his love of the arts led him to elevate himself to the rank of king, and his capital, Berlin, to a center of correspondingly greater splendor and culture. His son, Frederick William I (1713-1740), more like the Great Elector, resumed the congenial task of increasing his income and his army, but cared little for music, philosophy or literature. These, however, were precisely the subjects which most interested the next heir, Crown Prince Fritz, a fact which caused a most distressing domestic conflict between father and son. Fortunately, when Fritz became King as Frederick II in 1740, he had developed into such a many-sided genius that he was able to continue his youthful cultural interests, and at the same time rival his father in continuing the task of building up the army, the finances, and the administrative structure of the State. Moreover, whereas Frederick William I had generally avoided war because he could not bear to see his beloved battalions decimated in battle, Frederick the Great used the army to acquire new lands and power for his country and greatly increased prestige for himself as its king.

FREDERICK (III) I, 1688-1713

Frederick, the third Brandenburg Elector of that name, inherited the improved financial and military machinery and the able officials of the Great Elector. Consequently the revenues continued to rise for nine years; his credit was so good that he was able to borrow heavily; and there seemed to be plenty of money for his lavish expenditures. He joined at once with the armies of the Emperor and of William of Orange, in return for the promise of considerable subsidies, and helped drive the French out of Germany and the Netherlands. At the Peace of Ryswick, however, in 1697, he felt that his dignity was injured by the scant consideration with which he was treated by his allies and was indignant that he was rewarded with no territory. The blame for this he unjustly laid on his chief minister, Eberhard von Danckelman.

This remarkable man, who came from a Calvinist family in Münster, had been Prince Frederick's tutor, and for years enjoyed the Elector's absolute confidence and favor. Danckelman and his six brothers were appointed to numerous lucrative offices. Danckelman himself was given almost undisturbed control of the government. By 1697, however, he had aroused the envy of the nobles and other officials by his power and wealth. He had also aroused the enmity of the Electress, Sophie Charlotte, by his close hold over the purse strings and by an exclusive influence over her husband which she coveted for herself. Court intrigues, which sought to poison the Elector's mind against his all-powerful minister, triumphed, when Frederick convinced himself that Danckelman was to blame for humiliations at Ryswick, and especially when he found that Danckelman was opposed to his pet project of making himself King of Prussia. Danckelman feared the kingship would be opposed by the Emperor and other princes, and in any case would entail too expensive a royal court. On December 4, 1697, the all-powerful minister was suddenly dismissed from all his offices and soon brought to trial on unsubstantiated charges of corruption. The ungrateful king confiscated all his property and kept him in prison until 1707 after the death of Sophie Charlotte. Well might he exclaim with Schwartzenberg or Bismarck: "Put not your trust in princes!"

Frederick's desire for the kingship was whetted by seeing his neighbors raised in rank: the Duke of Brunswick was elevated to be Elector of Hanover in 1692, and his son already had the prospect of becoming George I of England; and the Elector of Saxony abandoned Lutheranism to become King of Poland in 1697. Frederick's opportunity came with the death of poor Carlos II of Spain on November 1, 1700; the Emperor was willing to buy the support of 8000 Brandenburg troops to secure his claim to the Spanish Succession by agreeing to recognize the royal title whenever Frederick should proclaim himself king in Prussia. Once the Emperor's consent was gained, Frederick lost no time. On January 18, 1701, in the presence of the Prussian

Estates assembled for the purpose, he placed a crown upon his own head and another upon that of his wife. To emphasize his independence of the Church, the coronation took place in the Königsberg castle; only afterwards did the royal procession then move to a chapel where the king and queen were consecrated by two Protestant bishops specially created for the occasion. To emphasize his position as sovereign prince outside the Empire and to avoid complications with Poland which ruled West Prussia, Frederick took the title King in Prussia (*Rex in Borussia*). At the same time, using the emblem of the old Teutonic Knights, he founded the distinguished Order of the Black Eagle, with their motto indicating just reward and punishment: *Suum cuique*. To regard the coronation as a mere act of vanity on Frederick's part would be a mistake. In an age when formalities counted for much, it marked a very real increase in the power and prestige of the Brandenburg-Prussian State, and gave it the rank in Europe to which the Great Elector's solid achievements entitled it. Though only king "in Prussia," Elector Frederick III was soon known as Frederick I, King of Prussia; people spoke of the "Royal Prussian Army"; and the administration in all his provinces was henceforth known as the "Royal Prussian Administration." The crown became a new symbol of unity.

Frederick also secured from the Emperor the privilege of having law-suits involving less than 2500 gulden exempted from appeal to the Imperial Courts. This did not apply to the Electorate of Brandenburg which by the Golden Bull of 1356 had long enjoyed a complete *privilegio de non appellando,* nor to East Prussia which lay outside the Holy Roman Empire. These two lands (and also Ravensberg) continued to have their local supreme courts (i.e., in Brandenburg the *Kammergericht*). For all his other lands Frederick I established in 1703 a new High Court of Appeal (*Ober-Appellationsgericht*) as a step toward the centralization of justice. By a further step in 1748, as a result of the reforms toward legal simplicity and uniformity of the great jurist, Cocceji, this court, commonly known as the High Tribunal (*Ober-Tribunal*), became a court of appeal for Brandenburg and Ravensberg as well as for the other provinces (except Prussia).

The Great Elector had done much for the improvement of Berlin, protecting it with defensive fortifications, providing fire protection and street lighting, laying out the Unter den Linden avenue and the Friedrich and Dorotheen settlements on either side of it, and establishing in his palace the valuable public library with rare oriental manuscripts which was to become, as the Prussian State Library, one of the half dozen greatest libraries of the world. Frederick I was ambitious to do much more. He enlarged the palace to substantially its present size (except the cupola). He built the massive arsenal (*Zeughaus*), now used as a museum of military history. He added seven churches to his capital. He imported Dutch and French engineers, architects, painters and musicians, but none of them left such a lasting mark on the baroque style of the period as his own famous architect and sculptor, Andreas Schlüter, who did the imposing equestrian statue of the Great Elector commanding the Long Bridge over the Spree.

Frederick's wife, Sophie Charlotte of Hanover, was a great help to him in making Berlin a cultural center. With unusual personal charm and with an interest in literature and philosophy which, however, was more lively than profound, she attracted to her court many notable men. Among them was the versatile genius Leibniz, famous as theologian, historian, philosopher and statesman, as well as for the discovery of calculus. He was made first president of the new Berlin Academy of Sciences, established in 1701, which combined in its aims the scientific interests of the Royal Society in London and the French Academy at Paris. For its endowment it was given a monopoly of the manufacture and sale of calendars, which happened at the moment to be rather lucrative as Frederick I had just dropped out eleven days and adopted the "New Style" of Pope Gregory XIII. This new Gregorian calendar, now in universal use throughout Christendom, had been dutifully accepted by most Roman Catholic countries in 1582, but foolishly rejected by most Protestant rulers for a half a century or so longer. The Berlin Academy suffered a blight under the unsympathetic austerity of Frederick William I, but under the patronage of Frederick the Great began to live up to the high hopes of its founder, and in the nineteenth century became one of the world's most distinguished learned societies. Sophie Charlotte's name is perpetuated in Charlottenburg, where Frederick I built another palace and where there gradually grew a pleasant residential suburb to the west of Berlin beyond the Great Elector's Tiergarten.

The University of Halle, dedicated in 1694 and provided with funds from the exploitation of the rich newly acquired salt deposits near by, together with the earlier universities at Frankfort on the Oder (1506), at Königsberg (1544), and at Duisburg in the Rhineland (1655), gave Frederick a seat of learning in each of his principal provinces. Halle soon became doubly

distinguished for its progressive jurisprudence and its
tolerant and practical theology in contrast to the narrow scholasticism and dogmatic Lutheranism or Calvinism of most of the German universities. Here Christian Thomasius (1655-1728) had the courage to defy
tradition by lecturing in German instead of in Latin.
He was a pioneer in restoring the German language as
a medium for scholars, gave a stimulus to the study of
Germanic Law in contrast to prevailing Roman Law,
and edited in German a legal magazine. He attacked
witchcraft trials and the use of torture, favored the the-
ories of Natural Law already developed by Grotius and
Pufendorf, and prepared the way for the Enlightened
Despotism of the eighteenth century. A. H. Francke
(1663-1727), besides teaching the new, lovable, Quaker-
like Christianity known as Pietism which was being
preached at Berlin by P. J. Spener (1635-1703),
aroused an interest in popular education in his Orphan
Asylum at Halle, and corresponded with Cotton Mather
at Harvard College. So from Halle came pastors, jurists and civil servants, trained with a progressive outlook in government and a broad toleration in religion,
who were of decisive advantage to the new Prussian
Monarchy.

THE WAR OF THE SPANISH SUCCESSION (1701-1713), AND THE SECOND NORTHERN WAR (1700-1721)

The fall of Danckelman in 1697 involved that of
Knyphausen and many other able officials, and opened
the way to dishonest favorites who wheedled Frederick
I by flattery and by finding money for his royal court
and the embellishment of Berlin. These favorites,
Wartenberg, Wartensleben, and Wittgenstein, later ex-

ecrated as "the three W[oes]," mismanaged the numerous offices which they assumed, enriched themselves, and piled up a state debt. The Household expenditure rose from quarter of a million talers in 1687 to nearly half a million in 1711. Foreign war and the pest and famine which swept over Europe in 1709 and the following years finally revealed the mismanagement and dishonesty of the king's incompetent ministers. An investigation, largely instituted by Crown Prince Frederick William, led to their downfall in 1711 and to reforms which became drastic as soon as Frederick William became king in 1713.

Meanwhile Prussia had been caught between two great wars. In the east the accession of the ambitious Charles XII of Sweden and his defeat of Peter the Great at Narva in 1700 opened the Second Northern War; he then turned back to conquer Poland and set up his camp in Saxony near the Prussian frontier. In the west the death of Carlos II and the rival claims of the French, Hapsburgs and Bavarians to his inheritance opened the War of the Spanish Succession; Dutch and English took a decisive part in this war when Louis XIV foolishly recognized the Stuart Pretender as King of England upon the death of William of Orange in 1702. What should Frederick I do?

Since Prussia's resources did not allow him to divide his efforts by intervening in both conflicts, Frederick had to choose. His true interests lay in the east where, by taking the side of the rising power of Russia, he had the prospect of acquiring Polish (or West) Prussia and Swedish Pomerania and of winning a strong position on the Baltic. But neither Charles XII nor Peter the Great were willing to pay the subsidies on which the Prussian army was more than ever dependent, owing to the financial mismanagement of Danckelman's successors. On the other hand, by taking up arms against Louis XIV, Frederick would fulfill his coronation agreement with the Emperor and continue the Great Elector's policy of protecting Germany and Protestant interests. Furthermore, he would probably promote his claims to the Orange family lands, and he felt that there was always safety in subsidies. So he chose the west, and on December 30, 1701, joined the Grand Alliance against Louis XIV.

In the War of the Spanish Succession Prussian "auxiliary forces" fought with distinction all over Europe— at Blenheim on the Danube under Marlborough, in Italy, on the Rhine, and in the Netherlands. At the Peace of Utrecht in 1713 Prussia acquired some bits of the Orange inheritance which Frederick I had annexed during the war: Mörs and Lingen in 1702, and Tecklenburg in 1707, near Cleves; Neuchâtel on the western border of Switzerland in 1707; and Upper Gelders in the Spanish Netherlands in 1713, as compensation for parts of the Orange inheritance which went to France.

In the Northern War Charles XII, drawn far from home into the depths of southern Russia, was defeated at Poltava in 1709 and fled to Turkey where he lived in helpless exile for five years. Meanwhile Russians and Poles invaded Swedish Pomerania, disregarding the neutrality of the Empire. Frederick I, with his troops in the west, could do nothing to defend Germany's eastern frontier. After his death on February 25, 1713, a few weeks before the Treaty of Utrecht was signed on April 11, his successor, Frederick William I, received a visit from Peter the Great in Berlin. Peter urged him to join in besieging the fortresses in Swedish Pomerania, but the king replied that he needed a year to put his army and finances in order. In October Peter bombarded and captured Stettin. As a gesture of respect for the neutrality of the Empire he agreed that Frederick William should hold Stettin in sequestration, pay the Russians 400,000 talers for war costs, and maintain the neutrality of Pomerania for the remainder of the Northern War. In 1714 this arrangement was suddenly upset by Charles XII. Dashing on horseback from Turkey to the Baltic, he threw himself into the Pomeranian fortress of Stralsund, and threatened Peter, Frederick William, and the neighboring German princes. Then at last Prussia took up arms. In alliance with the Danes she conquered Stralsund, Rügen and Wismar, while George I of England and Hanover seized the secularized bishoprics of Bremen and Verden which Sweden had held since the Thirty Years' War. After Charles XII had been killed in an attack on Denmark, the Northern War was gradually brought to a close by a series of treaties between 1719 and 1721. Frederick William I, by the Treaty of Stockholm (February 1, 1720), retained Stettin which he had held in sequestration for six years, acquired the eastern half of Swedish Pomerania stretching from the Oder to the Peene, and paid Sweden two million talers for it. Prussia now controlled both banks of the lower Oder and possessed in Stettin a first-class Baltic port.

FREDERICK WILLIAM I, 1713-1740

Born in 1688, Frederick William was brought up by a French nurse, a French tutor, and a Prussian noble of French ancestry, Count Alexander von Dohna. From these excellent people he learned to speak French as a mother tongue, but when he wrote it or Germanized it in the barbarous habit of the day he exercised a sovereign contempt for grammar and spelling. His German was coarse but vigorous. His innumerable royal comments on state papers, expressed phonetically, brutally, humorously and vehemently, stamp him as one of the most interesting, forceful, hard-headed and misunderstood of Hohenzollern rulers.

From his tutors also he received a Calvinistic reverence for God Almighty's power and a puritanic temper. This made him abhor the loose life and cabals of his father's court, and inspired his own reign with a sense of public duty as powerful as Kant's categorical imperative. He hated all shams, deceit, intrigues, and costly display (except in military matters), and was himself so naïvely free from these faults that he was sometimes taken in by others. He had by nature a violent temper which made him bring his cane down unmercifully upon his family and his subjects.

The king worked very strenuously himself and expected his civil servants to do likewise, "for I pay them to work"—though he did not pay them much; *travailler pour le Roi de Prusse* became proverbial for hard work and small pay. He was, however, at bottom genuinely kindhearted and solicitous for the well-being of his people. If he struck loiterers, grafters and people who got in his way or opposed him, he at the same time provided for poor widows, maintained a great orphan asylum at Potsdam, and continually warned lawyers and domain officers not to plague the people with long vexatious suits and unjust exactions. He was quick to scold and condemn, but also ready to pardon—especially if the offender happened to be one of his beloved soldiers. A musketeer who had stolen 6000 talers was sentenced by a judge to the usual penalty of the gallows; his colonel who did not want to lose a good fighter appealed to the king; Frederick William summoned the judge, knocked out a couple of his teeth with the ever-ready cane, and the musketeer went scot free.

Already as crown prince, Frederick William manifested the twin interests which were to characterize his reign: rigid economy and an imposing army. From his allowance, of which he kept a precise "Reckoning of my Ducats," he saved 50,000 talers, besides making generous church donations and building his favorite hunting-lodge at Wusterhausen. Here he made an excellent collection of military weapons of all sorts, and trained and equipped at his own expense a militia company of "big fellows." In 1709 he joined the Prussian troops in the War of the Spanish Succession, fought under the eye of Marlborough, was allowed to recommend officers for promotion and formed an intimate friendship with his father's ablest general, Field-Marshal Leopold von Dessau ("the Old Dessauer").

For a full quarter of a century, 1688-1713, from the cradle to the throne, the growing heir had seen his country involved in almost continuous war. To his chagrin he realized that Prussia's army, and consequently her whole foreign policy, was dependent on foreign subsidies. He resolved to make himself independent of subsidies, to build up a war-treasure of his own, and to have an army large enough to defend Prussia and to follow a policy in accordance with her own true interests. This was a policy of peace. With the brief exception of the tail-end of the Northern War, Frederick William kept his country out of war. At his accession in 1713 he inherited a bankrupt admin-

istration and an army of 40,000 men. At his death in
1740 he left his son a model administration in which
the annual domain revenue had risen from 1,300,000 to
3,300,000 talers, a war treasure of 8,000,000, and an
army of 83,000, regarded as the most efficient and best
disciplined in Europe. How did he do it?

ADMINISTRATIVE AND FINANCIAL REFORMS

More than two years before his accession Frederick
William had worked actively to get rid of some of the
worst abuses of the cabal administration of "the Three
Woes." It was largely owing to him that committees
of investigation were appointed in 1710. Their reports,
in spite of the efforts of the ministers to suppress or
belittle them, led to the downfall of Wartenberg, Wartensleben, and Wittgenstein. With their removal, the
supervision and keeping of all the domain and regalian
revenues was placed under a single able man, Ernst von
Kameke, who had the full confidence of the crown
prince. This consolidation of the civil revenue admin
istration was completed as soon as he became king by
the organization of a General Finance Directory and a
General Finance Chest. The former (*Generalfinanz-
direktorium*) took the place of the old *Hofkammer* created by Knyphausen and described above in Chapter
II. The latter (*Generalfinanzkasse*) swallowed up the
Chatulle which disappeared, and also the *general* revenues of the *Hofrentei* which sank back into a provincial Brandenburg *Landrentei*. The *Hofstaatskasse,* instead of continuing to receive a fixed revenue for the
Household, survived as a mere accounting institution
for it.

Frederick I's cabal ministers, before their removal

from office, had sought to raise ready cash by mortgaging the domains or by granting them out on hereditary leases, so that the domains were in danger of being virtually lost as a royal possession. This was stopped at once in 1711. Instead, there was a return to the Knyphausen system of leasing for a short term—usually six years, so that if the domains increased in value a higher rent might be charged when the lease was renewed. By these and other reforms, and by Kameke's strict and honest supervision, the domain revenues were almost doubled between 1711 and 1713.

Besides increasing the civil revenues, Frederick William I cut down drastically the civil expenditures so that the surplus might be used for the army. With filial piety he gave his father a gorgeous funeral such as he knew would have delighted Frederick I. Berlin saw its pomp and pageantry for the last time. Then, recognizing that Prussia was too poor to be both Athens and Sparta, the new king chose Sparta. Sending for the long list of court officials, he drew his pen through two-thirds of the names. Some of those dismissed were at once given places in the army. Those who remained had their salaries reduced to make them realize that he was now undisputed master and that if they were to have a raise again they must earn it by diligence and devotion. Thus the cost of the Household and administration was cut down by three-fourths—from 421,000 talers in 1711 to 102,000 in 1713. When he went to Königsberg to receive the homage of the East Prussian Estates, he covered the distance in four days with a modest retinue of 50 horses and spent 2547 talers. When his father had gone there for his coronation in 1701, he took fourteen days with a train of 2000 horses and spent 5,000,000 talers.

The ranking of the officials who were spared by Frederick William's pen was altered in accordance with his preference for soldiers over civilians. The gradations in rank, which had risen from 32 in 1688 to 142, were cut to 46. The High Chamberlain and the Grand Master of the Wardrobe at the head of the list disappeared altogether and were replaced by the Field-Marshal and generals; Privy Councilors were moved down from 5th to 6th place; and Major Generals were advanced from 19th to 9th, Colonels from 43rd to 19th, and Lieutenant Colonels from 67th to 33rd, etc. As the king said: "50,000 soldiers are worth more than 100,000 ministers."

All officials were to be inspired with a holy fear of the king's authority and with his sense of military devotion, discipline and punctuality. The Saxon Minister at Berlin, Manteuffel, reported:

Every day His Majesty gives new proofs of his justice. Walking recently at Potsdam at six in the morning, he saw a post-coach arrive with several passengers who knocked for a long time at the post-house which was still closed. The King, seeing that no one opened the door, joined them in knocking and even knocked in some window-panes. The master of the post then opened the door and scolded the travelers, for no one recognized the King. But His Majesty let himself be known by giving the official some good blows of his cane and drove him from his house and his job after apologizing to the travelers for his laziness. Examples of this sort, of which I could relate several others, make everybody alert and exact.

The military revenues were also increased. In East Prussia a new general land-tax (*Generalhufenschoss*) brought in a great deal more than the Great Elector's land-tax. It was also more equitable, because it was now for the first time levied upon the land of the nobles as well as upon that of the peasants. The excise was made fairly uniform throughout the kingdom, and, with the growing well-being of the people, rapidly augmented and even exceeded the land-tax. It was also used as a mercantilist measure for protecting and fostering Prussia's own manufactures at a time when the boundaries of the state were too irregular and extended to permit of an effective tariff frontier. Nobles who still held their land on feudal tenure were given their land in fee simple on payment of 40 talers; this commuted the military knights' service for which they were still theoretically liable, but which had no place in the new Prussian army. Instead of serving their feudal overlord by fighting as in the Middle Ages, the nobles now served the Prussian State by paying—by helping to support the army in which so many of them were engaged as officers.

The administration of the military revenues, which had been developed by Platen and his successors, was put in charge of a board known as the General War Commissariat (*Generalkriegskommissariat*). Its president was Friedrich Wilhelm von Grumbkow, an able and active man, who until his death in 1739 was one of Frederick William's most influential ministers. It supervised the Provincial Commissariats, which in turn supervised the local military tax-collectors (cf. p. 80). The latter, in their exercise of wide police power and of economic control in enforcing mercantilist measures, were active in stamping out the remnants of the provincial spirit of opposition of the Estates and in completing the work of establishing Prussian absolutism begun by the Great Elector.

THE GENERAL DIRECTORY OF 1723 AND CABINET GOVERNMENT

Frederick William found that the dual administration of the civil and military revenues gave rise to many painful conflicts between the General Finance Directory and the General War Commissariat, and especially between their respective subordinate officials. The domains officials represented primarily agrarian interests and wanted freedom of export for grain, wool and lumber. The Commissariat officials, on the other hand, were more concerned with fiscal, manufacturing, and restrictive mercantilist interests. Both groups, in their zeal to satisfy Frederick William's desire for more revenues, tended to encroach upon each other. To put an end to this "confusion," the king retired to a hunting lodge for the Christmas season and worked out a long "Instruction" which consolidated the hitherto separate civil and military revenue administrations under a single supreme board. This new body, established in January, 1723, rejoiced in the clumsy but unambiguous name of General Supreme Finance War and Domains Directory (*General-Ober-Finanz-Kriegs-und Domänen-Directorium*), commonly called for short the General Directory. It comprised four Departments whose heads were to report on their respective fields on certain days as follows:

1. Grumbkow (Mondays): Prussia, Pomerania; Frontiers and Agriculture.

2. Creutz (Wednesdays): Minden, Ravensberg; General Budget.

3. Krautt (Thursdays): Brandenburg, Magdeburg, Halberstadt; Army.

4. Goerne (Fridays): Cleves-Mark, Neuchâtel, Mörs, Gelders; Postal System and Coinage.

As is evident, the Departments were partly regional and reminiscent of the territorial growth of Prussia, and partly functional like the departments of government in a modern state. Each Department had no separate and distinct life of its own; it merely prepared the business assigned to it for consideration by the General Directory as a whole. Each of the four Department Ministers had three or four assistant colleagues who also sat and voted in the plenary session. Each Minister presided in turn on the day he presented his business, and then reported the discussion and resulting decisions to the king for his approval.

Under Frederick the Great five more Departments were added, all of which were functional and modern in character: a Department of Commerce and Industry (1740); of Army Supplies (1746) as a result of his experiences in the First Silesian Wars; and, in his reconstruction work after the devastation of the Seven Years' War, the Departments of Excise and Tolls (1766), Mines (1768), and Forestry (1770). Though Frederick William I's successors somewhat undermined the authority of the General Directory by the growing tendency toward "cabinet government" and by the appointment of "immediate commissions" to deal with special questions directly under the orders of the king, the General Directory of 1723, with some modifications, remained for four-score years the supreme governing board of the Prussian Monarchy until the reforms of Stein after the disaster at Jena.

In similar fashion Frederick William I consolidated the provincial domains and commissariat administrations into single collegial boards. Their members were forbidden to be residents of the provinces in which they served. This provision, as in the case of Richelieu's intendants in France, aimed to prevent officials from favoring friends and relatives. It was, however, in flat contradiction with the loudly demanded "right of the native born" of earlier days, and was significant of the way the fresh breeze of royal absolutism was sweeping away the sultry particularism of the Estates.

The central treasuries for the civil and military revenues (*Generalfinanzkasse* and *Generalkriegskasse*) were still kept separate because of the king's fear that military revenues might be diverted away from the army to other objects, as had happened under Frederick I. Under Frederick William I all revenues flowed into these two central treasuries. Frederick the Great, however, after 1763 assigned certain ordinary sources of revenue to each of these treasuries; thereafter, all new sources of revenue, such as the revenues from Silesia and from his new French tariff, coffee and tobacco monopolies, and so forth, flowed into a new *Dispositionskasse*. This third treasury, as its name implies, was at the private disposition of the king; he made expenditures from it without consulting his ministers—mainly expenditures for the army and for the amelioration of agriculture and industry after the impoverishment of the Seven Years' War. The income of this *Dispositionskasse* rose during the peaceful second half of his reign to exceed that of both the old treasuries. This system of uncontrolled personal royal expenditure worked well enough under an exact, energetic and shrewd genius like Frederick the Great, but was disastrous under his weak and spendthrift successor.

In order to get the basis for a general budget of all

his revenues and expenditures, Frederick William I set up in 1723 a Supreme Accounting Office (*Oberrechen-kammer*). It received and checked all the accounts. Its president was Creutz, who also, as Minister in charge of the Second Department of the General Directory, prepared the general budget.

Frederick William had declared that he himself would be President of the General Directory, in order to lend it "more luster, authority and impressiveness," but actually he almost never attended its meetings; the always empty presidential chair was merely the symbol of the supreme centralized authority which resided in the king. One of the reasons for this was that the General Directory sat in the Berlin Schloss, while Frederick William usually lived at Potsdam or at one of his hunting-lodges. Another reason was the growing tendency toward "cabinet" government at the expense of the Privy Council.

The Privy Council, after being for a century the supreme central board, had been gradually stripped of much of its business which was handed over to special individuals, commissions, or boards. Under Frederick I it met less frequently and was attended by only a few members; nor did the king usually preside in it as had been the Great Elector's regular habit when he was in Berlin. The consideration of foreign affairs, which had been one of the chief reasons for its foundation in 1604 and which for more than eighty years had formed one of its main items of discussion, was handed over after the fall of Danckelman to four Privy Councilors who formed a new *Staatskonferenz;* this was later sometimes known as the *Cabinetsministerium* and was the forerunner of the modern Ministry of Foreign Affairs.

Legal petitions and appeals to the Elector as the supreme fountain of justice, which for half a century had been dealt with in the Privy Council, were handed over in 1658, during the stress of business of the First Northern War, to four newly created councilors who with the Vice-Chancellor formed henceforth a Judicial Committee of the Privy Council, later known as the *Justizrat*. Other general questions, aside from foreign affairs, legal matters, and finance, were occasionally dealt with in the eighteenth century by a small group of select Privy Councilors forming what came to be known as the Privy State Council (*Geheimer Staatsrat*).

Under Frederick William I, and still more under Frederick the Great, the king tended more and more to decide matters personally himself in his private apartment or "Cabinet" and to issue orders by dictation to Cabinet Secretaries. The king no longer ruled *in* Council but *from* the Cabinet. This change became most marked under Frederick the Great whose residence at Sans Souci in Potsdam necessitated written communications with the administrative boards which sat in Berlin. This Prussian "Cabinet Government" (which of course had nothing in common with the English institution of the same name) marked the extreme form of centralization and absolutism, and made possible Frederick II's remarkable achievements as an Enlightened Despot. It worked well under such alert, intelligent, hard-working and conscientious monarchs as Frederick William I and Frederick the Great, but was to prove disastrous under their immediate successors during the storms of the French Revolution and Napoleonic invasion.

THE ARMY

Frederick William I has often been called The Royal Drill Sergeant. Certainly he gave a new spirit, discipline and efficiency to the institution which he had most at heart. He began by purging the officer corps of unworthy men, many of whom were foreign adventurers. Their places were given to his own nobles, who were forbidden to hire themselves out to other princes, according to the common practice of the day. For the instruction of their sons he founded a Cadet Corps at Berlin. This military employment of his own nobles helped to strengthen the bond between the nobility and the army and to wipe out the remnants of the old local opposition to the absolutist instrument of the new monarchy. The Junker nobility, proud of their class and accustomed to command the peasants on their landed estates, quickly developed in the army a strong *esprit de corps* and a sense of duty, discipline and social superiority which was thenceforth characteristic of the Prussian officer caste. They felt that the king, who after 1725 always wore a uniform, was one of their number.

The recruiting of the common soldiers lay, not with the higher military authorities, but in the hands of the captains who received a lump sum for enrolling and maintaining their companies. The recruiting officers often came into conflict with one another for men, and often used deceit or compulsion which led to protests, opposition and violence, especially when they attempted to get recruits from the lands of Prussia's neighbors. To remedy these abuses Frederick William adopted in 1733 the Canton System. The kingdom was divided into more or less equal districts or cantons, each of which was to supply the men for a particular regiment.

Soldiers were recruited mainly from the peasant class, served for a long period of years, and were therefore virtually a professional or mercenary army. The economic loss of withdrawing men from agriculture was much lessened by the king's provision that soldiers who had been once well drilled were released on furlough for nine months of the year; it lessened also the cost of maintenance and was naturally very welcome to the captains; only for short periods of spring and fall training were the companies brought up to their full numbers.

Frederick William I built some great barracks in Berlin and quartered many regiments in the various fortresses, but for the most part soldiers were lodged with families in the garrison towns. They either paid for their board or bought and prepared their own food, or had it done by their wives who frequently accompanied them. Instead of regarding the quartering of soldiers as an unwelcome burden, towns were glad to receive a regiment because the soldiers' expenditures stimulated economic life. Berlin increased in population under Frederick William I from 60,000 to 100,000, of whom 20,000 were soldiers.

The army was a little world by itself, with its own laws, justice and police. The soldier on furlough at home remained under the jurisdiction of his regiment and was not subject to the local court and police. Desertion was not uncommon; Frederick the Great advised generals not to take troops through a forest because it offered too good an opportunity for running away.

One of Frederick William's naïve hobbies was his

regiment of "Potsdam Giants." Composed of men well over six feet in height, and wearing a tall pointed headgear above their powdered heads, they formed one of the military sights of Europe. In addition to flint-lock and dagger, they carried a bag of hand-grenades, and hence were known as grenadiers. As Prussia could not furnish enough "tall fellows," they were recruited anywhere in Europe they could be found—a practice which involved the king in several diplomatic conflicts with his neighbors. Some astute rulers gained his goodwill by presenting him with giants; Peter the Great sent him several, and Frederick William returned the compliment by humoring the Tsar's pet hobby by the gift of a small yacht.

As the Potsdam Giants were expensive to recruit and maintain, Frederick William established a special Recruit Chest (*Rekrutenkasse*). Its revenues at first consisted of payments for royal acts of grace such as pardons and permission to marry within forbidden relationships, and also of a quarter of the first year's pay of newly appointed officers. This financial device was similar to the Great Elector's *Chargenkasse* (see above, p. 81), with which the Recruit Chest was merged in 1722. Anyone seeking an appointment to any civil office was advised to make a donation to the Recruit Chest; if the donation was not generous, the candidate was not likely to get the coveted appointment. This practice, which smacks of bribery and the sale of public offices, did not have such evil consequences as one might expect, because of the king's ever-vigilant eye for laxity or corruption in office. Frederick the Great restricted the practice and abolished the Potsdam Giants, believing that they were not worth what they cost and that men above normal size do not have more endurance or make better soldiers than men of average stature.

To improve efficiency, the wooden ram-rod, which was liable to break or catch fire, was replaced by an iron one. The bayonet, which had hitherto been fastened into the muzzle of the gun and had to be removed before firing, was now fastened outside the barrel, so that soldiers could advance close to the enemy and continue firing and then instantly use the cold steel without delaying to fix bayonets. A State gun-factory at Potsdam and a woolen mill at Berlin provided the army with a better single standard gun and proper uniforms. Frequent drills and maneuvers under Frederick William's exacting eye gave the troops quickness and precision of movement. These were extended by Frederick the Great into general autumn maneuvers and war games which gave the king the opportunity to judge the ability of his officers and to increase efficiency by weeding out the unfit and promoting the capable. He also developed the "oblique order" of attack, enabling a small army to defeat a much larger one by suddenly falling upon its flank.

By these improvements, as well as by his own genius for tactics and strategy, Frederick the Great was able to defeat half of Europe in the three Silesian Wars. At Hohenfriedberg in 1745, 58,000 Prussians routed 85,000 Saxons and Austrians, taking more than 7000 captives and 66 cannon. At Rossbach on November 5, 1757, 22,000 Prussians annihilated 43,000 Austrians, French and Imperialists; and just a month later, at Leuthen, 30,000 Prussians, by using the oblique order, rolled up 80,000 Austrians into a disastrous defeat.

Within fifteen years, in 1755, Frederick the Great doubled the army of 83,000 which he had inherited from his father. At the time of his death, in 1786, he had increased it to 200,000 men, and it was generally regarded as the best disciplined and most efficient fighting force in Europe.

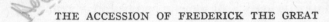

THE ACCESSION OF FREDERICK THE GREAT

Frederick the Great's life falls into three nearly equal periods: his youth and preparation for kingship until he was twenty-eight; the first half of his reign from 1740 to 1763 when he disturbed the peace of Europe by his three Silesian Wars; and the second twenty-three years of his rule when he sought to preserve the peace and *status quo* of Germany, lest he lose the Silesian prize which he had won. To be sure, in this third period he partitioned Poland and then waged the "Potato War" to prevent Joseph II of Austria from territorial aggrandizement, but essentially he aimed at peace, just as Bismarck a century later, having fought three wars to establish German Unity, became after 1870 a man of peace to preserve what he had secured.

Frederick's youth had been most unhappy and embittered. Loving music and French poetry, he had been forbidden these by his brutal prosaic father. Frederick hated his father's coarse family tyranny, his religious zeal, his financial stinginess, and his naïve submission to the intrigues of the Austrian minister who completely pulled the wool over his eyes. Frederick felt his situation to be so intolerable that he finally tried to escape to England. He was caught in the act. His father, in boundless rage, considered putting him to death as a deserter from the sacred Prussian army, but eventually listened to the Emperor's plea for mercy, and merely imprisoned Fritz in the fortress of Küstrin.

After a year Frederick William I's wrath cooled. He decided to give Fritz a chance to redeem himself by giving him command of a regiment and local administrative work. In this new life the crown prince did his best to live up to his father's military and economical standards. He even accepted with dumb filial obedience a wife selected for him by his father, at the instigation of the Austrian minister, who thereby prevented a marriage alliance between Prussia and England. Frederick was never really in love with his wife, never had any children by her, and after he became king ceased to live with her; but otherwise he treated her with respect and consideration.

In 1736 Frederick William I relented further, and provided his son and daughter-in-law with a pleasant estate at Rheinsberg to the northwest of Berlin. Here Fritz continued to win his father's esteem by the skill and success with which he managed the estate. In return he was allowed to indulge himself to his heart's content in music, literature and philosophy, and to have a select Round Table of cultured friends. The four years at Rheinsberg were the happiest of Frederick the Great's life. He read enormously, often sixteen or twenty hours a day. He stored his mind with classical French literature and with the writings of the Greeks and Romans in French translation. He took up philosophy, studied the campaigns of Caesar and Alexander the Great, and steeped his mind in the works of Machiavelli, Locke, Voltaire, Montesquieu, and Leibniz-Wolff. He wrote poetry, played the flute, and began a correspondence with Voltaire and other famous writers. His *L'Antimachiavel,* published anonymously in 1740, was a brilliant refutation of the Italian's principles of statecraft; it expressed Frederick's idealism and high moral philosophy—which he threw to the winds when dynastic interests and personal ambition impelled him to rob a defenseless woman of one of her richest provinces.

In these four happy Rheinsberg years Frederick made up for the deficiencies of his earlier education. He became one of the most cultured and best informed princes of Europe. Though he did not have the advantage of travel abroad, he had a far more accurate and enlightened knowledge of the lands and rulers of Europe than many more widely traveled persons. By hard study and the earnest application of a naturally brilliant mind, he matured himself to assume the duties of kingship. He learned to appreciate the sterling qualities by which his father, in spite of his crotchety tyranny, had built up for Prussia a large army and a substantial surplus treasure. And the father on his side regained complete confidence in his heir, declaring on the eve of his death on May 31, 1740, that he died content, "being sure of such a worthy son and successor."

Frederick II's first declaration of policy was an instruction to his civil servants that they were not to seek to enrich him by oppressing his subjects, but to have a single eye to the well-being of his country. He issued an edict abolishing torture, except in cases of treason and murder. He did away with the cruel practice by which mothers who killed their infants were sewn in sacks and drowned. He proclaimed absolute religious toleration, saying that all religions were equally good, provided their adherents were honest people, and that if Turks or heathen wanted to come and populate his lands he would build mosques and churches for them. He revived his grandfather's Academy of Sciences, appointed distinguished new members to it, and took an active personal part in its proceedings.   By such initial measures the philosopher-king announced the era of Enlightened Despotism which was to characterize his reign and of which more will be said later.

FREDERICK THE GREAT'S SILESIAN WARS, 1740-1763

Five months after Frederick II became king, Emperor Charles VI of Austria died unexpectedly at Vienna, on October 20, 1740, leaving a daughter, Maria Theresa, but no sons.   As a woman had never ruled in the Hapsburg lands, Charles VI had spent his last years in seeking to make sure that her succession would be everywhere recognized.   To effect this he had drawn up the "Pragmatic Sanction," which had been sworn to by the Estates of each of his lands and had been accepted by all of the principal European rulers including the King of Prussia.   No sooner had Charles VI died, however, than several princes, on one pretext or another, refused to recognize Maria Theresa's rights. The Elector of Bavaria laid claim to certain Hapsburg lands and even got himself elected Emperor in 1742. Frederick II, for his part, instantly decided to seize possession of the rich Hapsburg province of Silesia.

Frederick's motives were several.   He felt that Prussia had long been duped by Austria.   His father had been led around by the nose by the Austrian minister at Berlin who had reported to Vienna that Frederick William I was a poltroon who would never dare to fight.   Frederick II wanted to show that Prussia could assert herself as one of the great powers of Europe. He also burned to imitate the heroic deeds of which he had read so much, and thus win personal glory.

Therefore when he went to put himself at the head of his troops in Silesia, he left at home his most experienced general, old Leopold of Dessau, saying: "I don't want the world to say that when the King of Prussia goes to war he takes a tutor at his elbow." Moreover, the European situation seemed favorable: England was at war with France and Spain, and he believed that, in view of the long-standing enmity between the Bourbons and the Hapsburgs, he could secure France as an ally.

Frederick also saw the opportunity to make good claims which the Hohenzollerns had long had to half a dozen little counties in Silesia, but which the Hapsburgs had refused to recognize. Rather than negotiate for these in Vienna, he believed it shrewder to seize the whole of Silesia and negotiate afterwards. Silesia would form a very valuable acquisition of territory. Lying in the valley of the Oder, it had more than a million inhabitants, with thriving linen and other industries using the water-power from the little streams which flow from the Bohemian or Sudetes Mountains into the Oder. Though jutting out like an appendage to Brandenburg to the southeast, Silesia was really more closely connected with Brandenburg by the valley of the Oder than with Bohemia across the mountains to the west or with the Polish plains to the east. Two canals linked the Oder to the Spree, Havel and Elbe, with Berlin at the center of the water transportation system. As to Prussia's promise to respect the Pragmatic Sanction, that might be disregarded because Austria had not kept her promise to support Prussia's claims to Jülich and Berg, whose ruler had recently died without direct heirs. The legal claims to the half dozen little counties in Silesia were to Frederick of secondary importance; they were chiefly valuable as affording a plausible pretext to the world for his action. As he wrote to his Minister of Foreign Affairs, Pode-wils: "The legal question is an affair for you ministers, and it is time to work it up secretly, for the orders to the troops have been issued."

By the middle of December, 1740, the Prussian columns were on the march toward Silesia. On the 12th Frederick II gave a masquerade ball at the Berlin Schloss, and went from it to place himself at the head of his troops without giving the least hint of the stroke he had been preparing in secret for seven weeks. On the 16th, thinking of Caesar as he entered Silesia, he wrote joyously to Podewils: "We have crossed the Rubicon, with flags flying and music playing." The first weeks of the campaign were an easy military prom-enade for the young king and his troops, because Maria Theresa had been taken wholly by surprise and had only a few scattered garrison troops in Silesia. The strong fortress of Glogau was taken by assault on March 8. Breslau, the capital of Silesia, opened its gates in view of Frederick's promises of religious tolera-tion and the strict discipline maintained by his troops. His armies were then able to occupy the whole province.

By April, 1741, however, Maria Theresa had had time to recover from her surprise. Austrian troops filtered across the mountain passes from Bohemia into Silesia and threatened to cut off the widely scattered Prussian forces from their line of communications with Brandenburg. Frederick ordered his scattered troops to retreat quickly toward Breslau. On April 9 they found their way blocked near Mollwitz by an equal number of Austrians and rushed to attack. But the Prussian troops began to fire too soon, became disor-ganized, and appeared to be defeated. Frederick, rush-

ing forward, was in such imminent danger of being captured that his general, Schwerin, persuaded him to flee
to the rear. He spent a bitter, desolate night, riding
about trying to collect more troops. After he had left
the field, however, Schwerin managed to rally the Prussians and turned Mollwitz from a defeat into a victory.
It was a mortifying episode for the king who had set
out to win military glory and emulate Caesar and Alexander the Great. But it taught him valuable lessons:
that the field of battle is very different from the parade
ground; that actual fighting is necessary to make good
soldiers; and that a commander ought not to risk his
life at the forefront of his troops but stay toward the
rear to direct their movements.

The Prussian victory at Mollwitz was a surprise to
Europe. It had been generally expected that the Austrians would effectively punish Frederick for what was
regarded as a treacherous and foolhardy invasion. On
the day the battle was fought, Austria, Saxony and
Hanover had formed a coalition against him, and if he
had been defeated would probably have partitioned
some of his lands. Such was the political morality of
the eighteenth century. From an ethical point of view
Frederick was little better or worse than his neighbors.
He differed from them in that he was able to succeed
where they failed. The most important political result
of Mollwitz was that the French now decided to enter
into alliance with him, and soon sent an army to aid the
Bavarians in their attack upon Maria Theresa.

Strengthened by the French and Bavarians, Frederick was able to persuade the hard-pressed Austrians
to sign the Convention of Klein-Schnellendorf on October 9, 1741: Maria Theresa ceded to him most of
Silesia, and the Austrian troops, after a sham engage-

ment, were to withdraw from Silesia.   The Convention was to be kept secret to veil the fact that Frederick was leaving his allies in the lurch.   The Austrian troops were then free to occupy Bavaria and deprive the Elector of his own capital at Munich two weeks after he had been elected as "Emperor Charles VII."   Frederick, fearing that he might be attacked next, suddenly decided to reopen hostilities, alleging as a pretext that the Austrians had not kept the Convention of Klein-Schnellendorf secret as stipulated.   He invaded Bohemia and, by a brilliant flank attack on the Austrian left wing, won the Battle of Chotusitz on May 17, 1742. Leaving his allies again in the lurch, he then compelled Maria Theresa, by the Peace of Breslau on July 28, to cede the whole of Silesia.   This ended successfully for him the First Silesian War, but the general European War of the Austrian Succession, started by his action, was continued by the other participants until 1748.

Freed for the moment from the Prussian menace, Maria Theresa expelled the French and Bavarians from Bohemia, routed a second French army at Dettingen near Frankfort-on-the-Main in 1743, and was ready to attempt the reconquest of Silesia.   Fearing this, Frederick began a "preventive war" to crush her before she became strong enough to regain her lost province.   In this Second Silesian War of 1744-45 he invaded Bohemia through Saxony, but failed to capture Prag and had to retreat into Silesia for winter quarters.   In 1745 he purposely allowed the Austrians and Saxons to file through the mountain passes from Bohemia into Silesia. "If you want to catch a mouse, don't shut the mousetrap," he said significantly to a French friend.   Deceiving the enemy forces by a feigned hasty retreat, he suddenly advanced by a night march to a surprise attack at dawn. By eight o'clock on the morning of June 4, at Hohenfriedberg, 40,000 Prussians had completely routed 58,000 Austrians and Saxons, capturing 7000 prisoners and killing or wounding nearly 7000 more. Frederick's own loss was only 900 killed and some 4000 wounded. "The old Romans have done nothing more brilliant," he wrote to the faithful Podewils. In jubilation Frederick composed the "Hohenfriedberg March" and dedicated it to the Prussian army—a thoroughly creditable piece of martial music which has remained very popular in Germany ever since. After further victories Frederick entered Dresden, the Saxon capital, and there, on Christmas Day, dictated peace. Again Maria Theresa had to acknowledge him as the ruler of Silesia, and Saxony had to pay a million talers war indemnity.

During the next ten years he increased the army to more than 150,000 and gathered funds for a possible new war. Maria Theresa likewise reformed and enlarged her army, learning by the example of Prussia. She reorganized her government and finances in the direction of greater centralization, somewhat as the Hohenzollerns had been doing for a century. She made new secret alliances with Russia and Saxony, and by the "diplomatic revolution" was planning to ally herself with the ancient Hapsburg enemy, France, in place of the ineffective friendship with England. Frederick, scenting danger and knowing that France and England would always be on opposite sides, hastened to ally himself with England and abandon France.

In August, 1756, Frederick II opened the Third Silesian War by an unsuccessful attempt to invade Bohemia through the Saxon Mountains. The life-and-death struggle between Prussia and Austria which followed was only one part of the wider so-called Seven Years' War which was fought all over Europe, on the high seas, and in the colonies. Frederick had to face the larger part of Europe almost single-handed, because the English soon withdrew their promised subsidies and gave him no effective support. Though he won brilliant victories over French and German forces at Rossbach on November 5, 1757, and again over the Austrians at Leuthen in Silesia just a month later, the numerical odds were terribly against him, and the strain upon his nerves and resources was frightful. In the following years it was worse, because the Russians marched through East Prussia to the Oder and slaughtered thousands of Prussian soldiers in bloody encounters at Zorndorf in 1758 and at Kunersdorf in 1759. These were the black days when Frederick carried a vial of poison hidden on his person so that the King of Prussia should not be captured alive.

In 1762, however, the Russian danger was removed by the death of the hostile Empress Elizabeth and the accession of the friendly Peter III. Austria meanwhile was almost as exhausted as Prussia. As Maria Theresa's chief ally, France, had been everywhere defeated by England, she at last abandoned hopes of reconquering Silesia. By the Treaty of Hubertusburg on February 15, 1763, she renounced the rich province in favor of the Hohenzollerns for all time.

By the Silesian Wars Frederick had proved himself a military genius and an excellent administrator. To appreciate his tactics and strategy one should read the accounts in Thomas Carlyle's enthusiastic *History of Frederick the Great,* in the official Prussian General Staff History, or in Frederick's own *Histoire de mon*

Temps, Guerre de Sept Ans, and *Oeuvres Militaires.*
By his administrative skill he managed to finance the
wars without incurring foreign debts as did his neighbors. He did, to be sure, depreciate the coinage and
pay his bills in paper promises, but as soon as the war
was over he restored the coinage almost to its pre-war
value and redeemed the paper. He even came out of
the war with a considerable reserve in the war-chest,
from which he made a great many gifts or loans at low
interest to help "re-establish" his war-impoverished
subjects. Silesia, with its 1,180,000 relatively prosperous inhabitants, increased by nearly one-half the population of Prussia which in 1740 was still only about two
and a half millions. After 1763 the rich deposits of
coal, iron, lead, cobalt and other minerals in Upper Silesia began to be gradually exploited and to furnish an
increasingly large revenue. Silesia was allowed to keep
most of its local institutions. Instead of being placed
under the General Directory and integrated with the
rest of the Prussian administrative system, it was
placed under a special governor resident at Breslau and
directly responsible to the king.

By the Silesian Wars Frederick helped to overcome
the inferiority complex from which Germans generally
had suffered since the helpless, humiliating days of the
Thirty Years' War. By his brilliant victories, especially at Rossbach over the French, he had contributed
to the awakening of German nationalism which was
also beginning to find expression in the new German
literature of Herder, Lessing, Wieland and Klopstock.
He had raised Prussia to the level of the Great Powers
of Europe. People began to feel, as Mirabeau wrote in
1786: "Prussia is today, on the Continent, the pivot of
peace and war."

THE ACQUISITION OF WEST PRUSSIA, 1772

Frederick II returned to Berlin in 1763 tired in body and spirit, saddened by the strain imposed on his subjects by the war, and genuinely desirous of peace for the rest of his days.   It was as if a bleak, sunless winter's day had followed the spring-like warm enthusiasm and joyous self-confidence with which he had crossed the Rubicon in 1740.   He now realized poignantly how close he had come to complete disaster during the critical period of the Seven Years' War.   Deserted by England, he had had to fight single-handed on three fronts against Austria, France, Russia, and several German princes.   He had won, but he knew by how narrow a margin.   So, after being the chief disturber of the peace from 1740 to 1763, he now became its chief defender for the next twenty-three years.   For he realized that Prussia, occupying a dangerous middle position between the three continental great powers, and having a long, exposed and straggling frontier, was very vulnerable.   In another general war he might not escape disaster a second time.   After 1763, therefore, it was not he, but Catherine II of Russia and Joseph II of Austria who with their restless ambitions threatened the peace and *status quo* of Europe.   Frederick's aim was to hold them in check by skillful diplomacy.

How could Frederick break the ring of enemies encircling him?   Austria, smarting under the loss of Silesia, was likely to remain a potential danger.   She was still guided by the astute Kaunitz who had arranged the alliance with France and was soon to cement it further by the marriage of Maria Theresa's daughter to the French dauphin.   The French, moreover, had not forgotten that Frederick had thrice left them in the lurch. There remained Russia. The accession of Peter III in 1762 had been a heaven-sent piece of good luck for Frederick, but the next year Peter's wife profited by his assassination to mount the blood-stained throne as Catherine II. Coming from the little German principality of Anhalt-Zerbst which was overshadowed by Prussia, she at first disliked Frederick and began her reign by denouncing him as Russia's "mortal enemy." As heir to the policy of Peter the Great, she had great ambitions to extend her empire at the expense of Poland and Turkey, and thus threatened Frederick's policy of preserving peace and the *status quo*. Could he win her friendship without binding himself in an alliance with her which would involve him in an eastern war? He not only did so, but acquired another great province—at Poland's expense.

For a century Poland had been growing progressively weaker and was approaching a condition of chaos and anarchy. While the Hohenzollerns and Romanovs had checked the disintegrating tendency of the selfish nobility and had been building up a strong centralized government and princely absolutism in Prussia and Russia, a reverse process had been taking place in Poland. The Polish nobility had arrogated so many "liberties" to themselves that the king's power had shrunk to a shadow. The elective monarchy not only prevented any one dynasty from establishing its authority firmly, but invited bribery and interference by foreign powers at every election. The "Liberum Veto," by which any one Polish deputy could block legislation and "rupture" the legislature, and the "right of confederation," by which any group of nobles could band together for common political and military action against the rest, promoted and virtually legalized civil war. Fanatical Roman Catholic oppression of the "dissidents" offered Catherine and Frederick a pretext to intervene on behalf of their respective Greek Orthodox and Protestant co-religionists.

The death of Augustus III, King of Poland and Elector of Saxony, on October 5, 1763, opened a new Polish crisis. Catherine II desired the election of her former lover, Stanislas Poniatowski, believing that she could still keep him in her leading strings and through him as king could practically rule all Poland. By supporting her candidate, Frederick II saw an opportunity to win her goodwill and to protect his own lands. In an alliance of April 11, 1764, therefore, Frederick and Catherine agreed to guarantee each other's territories, to aid each other if necessary with troops, and to back the election of Poniatowski. This was harmless enough. But they went on to the cynical mutual promise that they would prevent any reforms in Poland which might strengthen the disintegrating state, such as the establishment of a hereditary in place of an elective monarchy and the abolition of the Liberum Veto.

Six months later, under Russian pressure, Poniatowski was duly chosen king in what was regarded as a remarkably peaceful election: "only ten men were killed." The new king, however, soon cast off Catherine's leading strings and sought to adopt a national policy for strengthening Poland. Catherine, seeing that her calculation of dominating Poland through her ex-lover had miscarried, began to make trouble for him. She instigated malcontent Polish nobles to form a "confederation" against him, stirred up a peasant revolt in South Poland, and demanded concessions for the Greek Orthodox dissidents. In 1768 she sent Russian troops to support the "confederation" opposing Poniatowski. These troops marched over a corner of Turkish territory, which threw the Grand Vizier into a paroxysm of rage and caused a six-year Russo-Turkish War in which Catherine was overwhelmingly triumphant on land and sea.

Frederick the Great disapproved of all these high-handed acts of Catherine II, but remained complaisant for fear of antagonizing his only friend. To be sure, as a hint to her that there were limits to his complaisance, he had a couple of friendly interviews with his admirer, Joseph II of Austria, who at this time was jealous of Russian expansion toward Constantinople.

As Austria and France did not want Catherine to retain all the lands she had occupied in the war with Turkey, what happier solution than to compensate her with a large slice of Polish territory, now that Poniatowski would no longer do her bidding? Austria had seized the Polish district of Zips in 1770. Polish Prussia, as Frederick had privately pointed out when he was only nineteen—in a letter to his friend, Natzmer, in 1731—would be a most valuable acquisition for the Hohenzollerns. Why not have all three of Poland's powerful neighbors take coveted slices of her defenseless territory as an easy solution of the Eastern Question? The subject was mooted between Catherine and Frederick's brother, Prince Henry, on his visit to St. Petersburg, and quickly resulted in the First Partition of Poland in 1772.

Catherine took White Russia and Lithuania; Maria Theresa, protesting with tears against the iniquitous proceeding, nevertheless took Galicia; and Frederick joyfully received the wedge-shaped Bishopric of Ermeland in East Prussia and Polish, or West, Prussia

though without Danzig and Thorn.   Though his share
was only one-third in size that of Catherine and one-
half that of Maria Theresa, it was politically more
important.

The Partition gave Frederick II control of the valley
of the Vistula highway.   It united the eastern and central Hohenzollern lands in a solid continuous territory
by connecting East Prussia with Pomerania and Brandenburg.   It not only freed Prussia from the danger of
further Russian attacks through Poland, but, since
Prussia had now become *particeps criminis* with Russia
in dismembering Poland, the Hohenzollerns and Romanovs were henceforth drawn together politically for
more than a century by their common interest in pre-
venting any restoration of Poland.   It also increased
Prussia's population by some 600,000 inhabitants,
partly Germans, partly Poles, and partly doubtful Cas-
subians.   Prussia recovered a territory which had been
conquered and settled by the Teutonic Knights, but
which had been taken from the Germans at their time
of weakness and defeat in 1466.   On the other hand,
it increased the bitterness between Germans and Poles,
which did not cease when this so-called "Polish Corridor" was restored to Poland in 1919.

THE "POTATO WAR" OF 1778-1779, AND THE LEAGUE OF PRINCES

Joseph II became Emperor of the Holy Roman Empire and joint-ruler with his mother, Maria Theresa, in
1765. An Enlightened Despot like Frederick II and
Catherine II, he was eager to reform and strengthen
his miscellaneous lands and play a leading rôle.   In
1778, upon the death of the Elector of Bavaria without

direct heirs, he made a secret treaty with the next Wittelsbach claimant, Charles Theodore of the Palatinate, who had no legitimate children but plenty of illegitimate ones of whom he was personally fond. Joseph agreed to provide pensions for the bastards, and in return was to get a third of Bavaria, which he at once occupied with troops. But another Wittelsbach heir, Charles of Zweibrücken, protested the arrangement which would deprive him of some of his ultimate inheritance. Alone, he was helpless.

Frederick the Great, however, immediately championed the rights of Zweibrücken and stood forth as the Defender of the Germanic Constitution and the *status quo*. Under cover of generous disinterestedness, he wished to prevent such an increase of Austrian territory and power as would upset the balance in Germany and possibly encourage Joseph II to attempt to recover Silesia. When Joseph paid no heed to his demands for the withdrawal of Austrian troops from Bavaria, Frederick sent a Prussian army under his brother into Bohemia. Owing to lack of energy and to mistakes, Prince Henry avoided battle. Both armies merely maneuvered until winter came on, when the Prussians withdrew again into Silesia. The soldiers, who had been occupied chiefly in finding provisions, derisively dubbed this War of the Bavarian Succession the "Potato War." In the following year, Russia and France, allies respectively of Prussia and Russia, mediated a compromise settlement by the Peace of Teschen of May 13, 1779. Austria kept the Innviertel, a small corner of Bavaria east of the Inn, but withdrew her troops and abandoned all claims to the rest of the Bavarian inheritance. Frederick had essentially succeeded in his main purpose of thwarting any great increase of Hapsburg power.

In 1780, with the death of Maria Theresa, Joseph II became sole ruler of Austria and was more free to indulge in his revolutionary enterprises. By visiting and flattering Catherine II, and by planning with her a joint spoliation of Turkey, he secured her favor just as Frederick began to lose it by his pro-Turkish attitude. Encouraged by this shift in the European diplomatic situation, Joseph II suddenly announced in 1784 his bold project of giving the complaisant Charles Theodore the far-away, restless Austrian Netherlands and receiving from him in exchange the contiguous Bavarian Electorate. Again Charles of Zweibrücken protested, and again Frederick the Great championed his rights, this time not by force as in 1778, but by the formation of a League of Princes (*Fürstenbund*).

The *Fürstenbund*, composed at first of the three principal north German states—Prussia, Saxony and Hanover—was soon joined by fourteen others, great and small, Protestant and Catholic. Its purpose was to protect the Germanic Constitution and the *status quo*. Supported diplomatically by France, which by the Peace of Westphalia was also one of the guarantors of the Germanic Constitution, it effectively blocked Joseph II's high-handed Bavarian Exchange Plan. It has sometimes been represented as a first step in the Prussian unification of Germany which was to be achieved later by Bismarck. In reality, the *Fürstenbund* did not aim at the creation of a new nation but the conservation of an outworn medieval mosaic, by winning to the side of Prussia other German princes who were frightened by Joseph II's revolutionary ambitions. It was Frederick's final diplomatic success. On August 17, 1786, the lonely old man, idolized as "Der Alte Fritz" by the masses, if not by the hard-worked soldiers and officials, closed his eyes at Potsdam, little dreaming how the revolutionary flood from France was soon to sweep away what he had attempted to conserve.

FREDERICK THE GREAT AS ENLIGHTENED DESPOT

Frederick II, whom other monarchs and their ministers of the latter eighteenth century sought to emulate, was the most distinguished representative of what is called Enlightened Despotism. This was based on the idea that the king, having studied the enlightened doctrines of the *philosophes*, knew better than his subjects what was for their good, and that he had, or should have, the despotic power to carry out reforms, not for his own glory, but for the well-being of his people and the advantage of his State.

"I am the first servant of the State," was Frederick's oft-repeated motto. When a delegation of townspeople came to thank him for a generous donation of money which he had made to enable them to rebuild their houses destroyed by fire, Frederick, "visibly moved," replied characteristically: "You have no need to thank me; it was my duty; that is what I am here for." The justification of his absolute authority, he believed, did not rest upon the Grace of God, Divine Right, or dynastic inheritance, but upon the Natural Law theory of the Social Contract—upon his ability to serve his people better than they could serve themselves.

The Enlightened Despotism of the latter eighteenth century thus stands as a transition between the seventeenth century Absolutism as typified by Louis XIV and the nineteenth century Democracy which was introduced on the Continent by the French Revolution. Louis XIV exalted his own personal glory, considering himself the source of all radiance and light, and choosing as his symbol the Rising Sun like that of a modern stove polish advertisement. He constituted the whole State according to the maxim which Voltaire put into his mouth: *L'état, c'est moi*. His will was law: *Si veut le Roi, si veut la Loi*. In the well-being of his subjects, whom he exhausted by long wars and oppressed with heavy taxation, he took relatively little interest. His government was neither *by* the people nor *for* the people.

Frederick the Great, on the other hand, as Enlightened Despot, marked a great step forward. He distinguished between himself as the servant of the State and the Prussian State itself. "The Ruler is the first servant of the State; he is well paid so that he may uphold the dignity of his position." Like Montesquieu, he believed that the monarch was subject to the law. In his *Political Testament* of 1752 he wrote: "I have resolved never to interfere with the course of legal procedure; for in the halls of justice the laws shall speak and the monarch shall keep silence." In the famous Miller Arnold case, where he broke this resolution, he did so because he believed—incorrectly—that a noble, backed by unjust judges, had done a great wrong to a poor peasant. If he exacted oppressive taxes, he did not spend them on costly robes to replace his simple blue uniform, soiled with dust and snuff, but returned a large part of them, even amounting to a quarter of his revenues in the years following the Seven Years' War, in free gifts for the amelioration and well-being of his subjects. His reforms, imposed with moderation from above, served in some sort as a lightning-rod which drew off discontent and averted in Prussia violent reform by the masses from below, such as took place in France soon after his death. His was a government *for* the people, if not *by* the people. He was nearer than Louis XIV to the nineteenth century and to Lincoln's conception of a "government of the people, by the people, for the people."

Frederick was a man of action rather than an organizer. He did not greatly change the framework of centralized institutions which he inherited from his father. He did, however, in actual practice gather much more power directly into his own hands, and left less freedom of action to his ministers. The members of the General Directory rarely reported to him in person, or even saw him, except once a year when the budget was drawn up. The reports of the various boards sitting in Berlin were sent to him at Sans Souci in Potsdam in writing, and he gave his decisions by dictating to his cabinet secretaries or by jotting down marginal notes from which they prepared his "Cabinet Orders." The amount and variety of the business which he thus dealt with is almost incredible. A fraction of it which has been published fills forty-four volumes of his *Politische Korrespondenz* and a score of volumes of the *Acta Borussica*. His working day began at 6 A.M. In the evenings he sought recreation in music, playing the flute to the Round Table of select friends; or in reading, in discussing philosophy, or in catching up on his literary writings and correspondence which comprise the thirty-three volumes of his *Oeuvres*.

In addition to this daily routine at Sans Souci and to commanding his troops in the Silesian Wars, Frederick

made frequent journeys of inspection through his provinces. He talked with nobles, burghers, peasants and
local officials, noting down with neat precision all sorts
of statistics in the little red leather notebooks which
he always carried with him. This information gathered
on the spot enabled him to check up on the reports of
his ministers, spend money where he was convinced it
was needed, and inspire everywhere his own sense of
duty and hard work. If his sharp eye detected corruption, incompetence or insubordination, instant dismissal
and a year's imprisonment at Spandau were likely to be
the offender's fate.

Frederick II's minute personal direction of every
branch of the government had its advantages. Decisions by the king were far more speedy than by majority votes after long discussions by boards of ministers.
Secrecy, where desirable, could more easily be maintained. All responsibility was centered in himself. As
in his campaigns he never called a council of war, so
in administration in general he saw no need for similar
assemblies for discussion and advice. By his example,
by his extraordinarily wide knowledge and mastery of
detail, and by the fear of disapprobation which he inspired he carried further his father's work of educating
Prussian military officials and civil servants to severe
standards of duty, honesty, efficiency and impartial
justice which for a century and a half were to make the
army and the bureaucracy the two solid pillars of the
Prussian State. His system, however, had also its dis-
advantages. It could be completely successful in the
long run only if his successors equaled him in genius—
which was not the case. Like Bismarck, he expected
obedience, not initiative and independent responsibility,

in his officials. He did not develop ministers of outstanding ability who could take over his autocratic machinery of government when his guiding hand was removed, nor did he try to provide a machine which would run itself, as a representative democracy is supposed to do.

With the disappearance at the Reformation of the clergy as one of the "three estates" of the Middle Ages, the nobles, burghers, and peasants came to form the three-fold division of society in Brandenburg-Prussia. This division was retained by Frederick II, and even sharpened by his social measures and by the provisions of his Prussian Law Code.

The nobility, instead of offering a narrow-minded local opposition to the Hohenzollern centralized monarchy, had now become its main and loyal support. No longer fearing the selfish political ambitions of the Junkers, Frederick extended their powers and privileges. In his name they exercised wide police powers on their landed estates. They were appointed more exclusively to officer positions in the army, for Frederick believed that they had a higher sense of honor than the middle and lower classes, and in any case they were used to commanding the peasants on their estates who formed the bulk of the recruits for the army.

The burghers were expected to serve the State, not by fighting, but by increasing its wealth through industry and trade. Consequently, after the Seven Years' War, they were not appointed officers and were exempted from being recruited as soldiers under the cantonal system. To promote internal trade and industry, Frederick II followed the usual mercantilist methods of excluding foreign manufactures by tariffs and by restricting the exportation of raw materials. He also swept away many internal tolls, especially those on the Oder which with the acquisition of Silesia had now become a water highway wholly within the Prussian boundaries. He established new monopolies for tobacco, porcelain, silk and other manufactures. He stimulated other industries by generous subventions from his *Dispositionskasse*. With the assistance of his able Minister of Mines, Heinitz, he began to develop the mineral resources of Upper Silesia. Ship-building began to flourish at Stettin; in a single year twenty ships were launched, some of which were sold abroad. In 1765, with the advice of an Italian, Calzabigi, he founded a Prussian Bank with a capital of 400,000 talers to aid recovery after the Seven Years' War. It received deposits, made loans, discounted paper bills, and later issued paper money. By 1786 it was making an annual profit of 22,000 talers.

According to statistics furnished by Heinitz in 1783, Prussia's annual exports amounted to 14,800,000 talers and her imports to 11,800,000, making a favorable balance of 3,000,000. Her manufactures had a total annual value of 29,000,000 talers, as follows:

Manufactures (*not including Silesia*)	*Workers*	*Home Consumption* (*value in talers*)	*Exported*
Silk	5,055	1,356,702	531,026
Woolens	39,367	3,344,166	1,691,305
Linen	22,523	373,506	897,757
Leather	3,595	996,614	399,986
Cotton	4,503	540,056	106,765
Iron and glass	8,373	2,126,675	1,053,844
Totals	83,416	8,737,719	4,606,683

Total home consumption and exports,
  approximately 13,500,000
Paper, tobacco, sugar, porcelain, tallow, soap . 4,500,000
Silesian woolens, linen, iron, steel, lead, etc. ..11,000,000

Total Prussian manufactures 29,000,000

In spite of this considerable industrialization under Frederick the Great, which raised Prussia to be the fourth manufacturing country of the world, Prussia still remained essentially an agrarian state, and the peasantry still bore the chief burden of the political and social order. Their sons were recruited for the rank and file of the army, which had increased to 200,000 in 1786. The heavy military land-tax was assessed exclusively on peasant land-holdings, except in East Prussia and Silesia where the land of the nobles also bore a part. In addition, the peasants had to perform labor services of three or four days a week for their overlords, not to mention services to the State such as building roads, transporting troops, and doing errands for officials and army officers. The peasant was, as Frederick the Great said, "the beast of burden of human society."

Frederick II attempted to do something to ameliorate the peasants' hard lot. On his own domain lands, which constituted about a third of the kingdom, he succeeded in assuring them heredity of tenure, in limiting in writing the nature and amount of their labor services, and in some cases in abolishing the obligation of menial service on the part of the peasants' sons and daughters. On the private estates of the nobles, however, he found that traditional custom and bitter opposition on the part of the Junker landlords were too strong for him to accomplish much. The only important reform he was able to achieve here was the prevention of *Bauern-legung,* i.e., the prying of the peasant off of his tenement so that the lord might add the peasant's acre strips to his own demesne lands.

To improve agriculture Frederick sent agents to England to study the better methods coming into use there. As a result he taught his own subjects to make greater use of fodder crops and of clover which enriched the soil instead of impoverishing it. It also made possible more feeding of cattle in the stalls instead of in the fields, improved the quality and amount of milk, and produced more stable manure which could be used further to enrich the fields. He persuaded his people to make greater use of such cheap forms of food as potatoes and turnips. He adopted better methods of cattle breeding, so that the number of sheep was increased from 5,500,000 in 1765 to 8,000,000 in 1786, making possible a considerable export of wool.

Frederick II began the systematic planting and care of pines and firs which gave Germany a leading place in modern forestry methods. To increase available agricultural land, he carried out extensive drainage projects, especially in the regions of the lower Oder and Vistula. These two rivers were connected by the Bromberg canal, thus making a direct east-west cheap water transportation between East Prussia and the central provinces. Like the Great Elector who settled 20,000 French Huguenots, and like Frederick William I who provided traveling expenses, land and live-stock for an equal number of exiled Salzburg Protestants, Frederick the Great was very active in colonization work. Not having at hand any such convenient bands of religious exiles, he sought his colonists in little groups from all over Germany and from neighboring foreign lands. In the course of his whole reign he far exceeded the work of his predecessors by settling a total of 300,000 colonists.

Frederick's grain policy was much the same as that of the Great Elector, but was pursued on a much larger scale. Generally the exportation and importation of grain was forbidden, though he sometimes allowed his own grain officials to import under cover from Poland. With the frontiers generally closed to grain, Frederick bought up and stored in government warehouses wheat, barley and rye in plentiful years when the price was low, and sold it again in years of bad harvest when prices tended to rise and would otherwise have caused great hardship to consumers. In this way he succeeded in his aim of keeping a fairly stable price level for grain and at the same time made a handsome profit.

In the intervals between his wars, and partly to aid recovery by public works, Frederick built many of the public buildings which have a prominent place in central Berlin today. The Opera House in 1743 was one of the first. Near it, on the same side of the Unter den Linden promenade, he constructed a library to house the growing collection of books which the Great Elector had started, and, a little to the rear, the Church of St. Hedwig for his Roman Catholic subjects. Across the Linden from the Opera House he erected a large palace for his brother, Prince Henry, which is now occupied by the University of Berlin.

One of Frederick's most important achievements was the reform and codification of the law. His father had made efforts at legal reform, but he had been too impatient, too ignorant of the fundamental difficulties, and too strongly opposed by the Junker justices to accomplish much. Frederick's success was largely due to Samuel von Cocceji. This able lawyer and skillful organizer had been dismissed by Frederick William I, but was restored to office by Frederick the Great. He raised the quality of the judges by giving them better pay, instead of having them largely dependent on gifts from the litigants. He simplified the long and costly Roman written procedure by restricting appeals and by making greater use of the Germanic oral procedure. He made use of the period of his enforced idleness, after his dismissal by Frederick William I, in drafting a code of simplified law to harmonize the practice in the different provinces. In 1751 he translated his Latin draft into German. During the next forty years other eminent lawyers and judges worked on it, and it was the basis of the Prussian Code finally put into practice in 1794.

Frederick the Great's reign is the culmination of a century and a half of extraordinary development of the Brandenburg-Prussian State. From a weak Electorate it had risen to be the strongest military state in Europe, with a population little smaller than that of England. A glance at four of the factors which the eighteenth century regarded as decisive for state strength will show the striking progress in this century and a half from the end of the Thirty Years' War to the death of Frederick the Great:

	1648	1740	1786
Population	750,000	2,500,000	5,000,000
Army	8,000	83,000	200,000
Annual revenues, in talers	?	7,000,000	19,000,000
Stored treasure, in talers	0	8,000,000	51,000,000

Under Frederick the Great Prussia had become the powerful rival of Austria, and, by accentuating the dualism in the Holy Roman Empire had, in spite of Frederick's efforts at conservation, actually hastened the disruption of that decaying medieval structure.

The Great Elector and Frederick William I had been fertile in creating new institutions and in organizing the resources of their lands. Frederick the Great added valuable new lands, but created little that was new in the way of institutions, being content to use and develop those which he inherited. However, by his demonic energy, his shrewd estimate of Prussia's interests, and his successful opportunism, he did more than either of his predecessors to raise Prussia high in importance as a European State. But Prussia still remained a despotic State, such as was characteristic of the eighteenth century. Unfortunately Frederick's genius as an Enlightened Despot was not a heritable quality to be transmitted to his immediate successors. It required the shock of the Napoleonic conquest and the genius of Freiherr vom Stein to bring about a new creative period of institutional changes which were to regenerate and further strengthen Prussia in the nineteenth century.

BIBLIOGRAPHICAL NOTE

GENERAL WORKS

In the following bibliographical suggestions no attempt can be made to indicate the vast material in German. Attention is called rather to books in English and French and a few German works of outstanding importance.

For a full list of works on German, as well as Prussian, history, the reader should refer to the comprehensive bibliography of F. C. Dahlmann and G. Waitz, *Quellenkunde der Deutschen Geschichte* (9th ed., Leipzig, 1932); the complete list and critical summaries of new books in the annual *Jahresberichte für deutsche Geschichte* (ed. A. Brackmann and F. Hartung, Leipzig, 1923 ff.); and the excellent articles and book reviews in the *Forschungen zur Brandenburgischen und Preussischen Geschichte* (Berlin, 1888 ff.) and *Historische Zeitschrift* (Munich and Berlin, 1859 ff.).

For art and architecture, fine illustrations, reproductions of old prints, together with excellent historical articles, the sumptuous annual folio, *Hohenzollern Jahrbuch* (Leipzig, 1897 ff.) is very attractive.

Of the general histories of Prussia the best is A. Waddington, *Histoire de Prusse* (2 vols., Paris, 1911-22), scholarly, very readable and well arranged, but comes only to 1740. The best German shorter account is O. Hintze, *Die Hohenzollern und ihr Werk* (Berlin, 1915), especially valuable for social and institutional history. A propagandist pamphlet of gigantic dimensions and prodigious research, from which all recent writers draw much material, is J. G. Droysen, *Geschichte der Preussischen Politik* (5 parts in 14 v., Leipzig, 1855-86); it aimed, by showing the superi-

143

ority of Prussia over Austria, to promote the unification of Germany under Prussian leadership as accomplished by Bismarck, but breaks off at 1757 with the author's death in 1884. A good corrective to Droysen, with many merits of its own, is H. Prutz, *Preussische Geschichte* (4 v., Stuttgart, 1900-02). H. Tuttle, *History of Prussia* (4 v., Boston, 1884-96) gives attention to institutions, is somewhat dull and unsympathetic, and, like Droysen, stops in the middle of the Seven Years' War owing to the author's death. Leopold von Ranke, *History of Prussia* (3 v., London, 1847-48), conservative and Lutheran in point of view, is still useful as political history. The first volume of Thomas Carlyle's *History of Frederick the Great* (6 v., London, 1858-65) gives a piquant and often amusing survey of his hero's predecessors for six centuries.

For the constitutional and legal history of Germany as a whole the best manual is R. Schröder, *Lehrbuch der deutschen Rechtsgeschichte* (6th ed., Leipzig, 1922). The Brandenburg-Prussian electoral and royal edicts, systematically classified, were edited by C. O. Mylius, *Corpus Constitutionum Marchicarum* (8 v. in folio, Berlin and Halle, 1736-41). The political views and testamentary instructions of Hohenzollern rulers are printed with comments by H. von Caemmerer, *Die Testamente der Kurfürsten von Brandenburg und der beiden ersten Könige von Preussen* (Munich and Berlin, 1915). O. Hintze, a master in the field of the institutional and social history of Prussia, has thrown much interesting light on the development from the Reformation to the French Revolution in his *Historische und Politische Aufsätze* (4 v., Berlin, 1908).

The survey of financial institutions by A. F. Riedel, *Der Brandenburgisch-Preussische Staatshaushalt* (Berlin, 1866) is valuable for its full statistical tables of receipts and expenditures from 1608 to 1806.

The organization and the development of the army, with some account of military history, is definitely treated by

C. Jany, *Geschichte der Königlich Preussischen Armee* (4 v., Berlin, 1928-33).

CHAPTER I

In addition to the general histories of Prussia mentioned above, one of the best surveys to 1648 is R. Koser, *Geschichte der brandenburgischen Politik* (Stuttgart and Berlin, 1913). G. Schmoller, *The Mercantile System and its Historical Significance* (New York, 1896) shows how economic and political factors went hand in hand in the struggle by which the Electors triumphed over local opposition. Interesting side-lights on Brandenburg-Prussia from the Roman Catholic point of view are to be found scattered through J. Janssen, *History of the German People at the Close of the Middle Ages* (17 v., London, 1896-1925).

The political and social organization of the Brandenburg Household and Administration in the later Middle Ages is given in admirable detail in H. Spangenberg, *Hof- und Zentralverwaltung der Mark Brandenburg im Mittelalter* (Leipzig, 1908), and in G. Schapper, *Die Hofordnung von 1470* (Leipzig, 1912). On the Reception of the Roman Law, see S. B. Fay, "The Roman Law and the German Peasant," in *Amer. Hist. Review*, XVI, 241-254, Jan., 1911.

The organization of the Estates in the sixteenth century is admirably described by M. Hass, *Die kurmärkischen Stände* (Leipzig, 1913); and the proceedings and debates of the Estates in their struggle with Joachim II, throwing a great deal of light on social, economic, and religious, as well as constitutional and financial matters, are printed by W. Friedensburg, *Kurmärkische Ständeakten* (2 v., Leipzig, 1913-16).

The beginnings of the Privy Council of 1604 and the preparations for the acquisition of Prussia and Cleves-Mark are well set forth in O. Hintze's article, "Kalvinismus und

Staatsräson in Brandenburg zu Beginn des 17. Jahrhunderts" in *Historische Zeitschrift*, 144: 229-286, 1931, and in the proceedings of the Privy Council which have been published for the years 1604-8 by M. Klinkenborg, *Acta Brandenburgica* (4 v., Berlin, 1927).

The activity of the Teutonic Order in colonizing Prussia is briefly told by J. W. Thompson, *Economic and Social History of the Middle Ages* (New York, 1928) and by E. F. Henderson, *Short History of Germany* (2 v., New York, 1902), and more fully by K. Lohmeyer, *Geschichte von Ost- und Westpreussen* (Gotha, 1888; 3rd ed., 1908).

<h2 style="text-align:center">CHAPTER II</h2>

A century of German history, with Prussia's prominent part in it, is admirably set forth in the well-illustrated Oncken Series by B. Erdmannsdörffer, *Deutsche Geschichte, 1648-1740* (2 v., Berlin, 1892-3); an introductory chapter describes the general effects of the Thirty Years' War.

The standard biography of the Great Elector is by M. Philippson, *Der Grosse Kurfürst Friedrich Wilhelm von Brandenburg* (3 v., Berlin, 1897-1903). For good shorter accounts, see the illustrated biography by E. Heyck, *Der Grosse Kurfürst* (Bielefeld and Leipzig, 1902), and the chapters by A. W. Ward in the *Cambridge Modern History* (New York, 1908, vol. V, chs. 20, 21, with bibliography).

The social and economic conditions in Brandenburg at the close of the Thirty Years' War are summed up in the introductions to the Privy Council Records edited by O. Meinardus, *Protokolle und Relationen des Brandenburgischen Geheimen Rates* (7 v., Berlin, 1889 ff.); these documents, which have been published for the years 1640 to 1667, are a mine of interesting information for every aspect of the Great Elector's internal administration.

His struggle with the Estates to establish his absolutism

can be followed in detail in the other chief documentary publication for his reign: *Urkunden und Aktenstücke zur Geschichte des Kurfürsten Friedrich Wilhelm von Brandenburg* (23 v., Berlin, 1864 ff.; vols. 5, 10, and 15-16 deal respectively with Brandenburg, Cleves-Mark, and East Prussia). The fatal opposition of Roth and Kalckstein is interestingly recounted by O. Nugel, "Der Schöppenmeister Hieronymous Roth" in *Forschungen zur Brandenburgischen und Preussischen Geschichte*, XIV, 393-479, 1901; by J. Paczkowski, "Der Grosse Kurfürst und Christian Ludwig von Kalckstein," *ibid.*, II, 407-513; III, 272-280, 419-463, 1889-90; and by F. Hirsch, "Zur Geschichte Christian Ludwigs von Kalckstein," *ibid.*, III, 248-271; V, 299-310. See also the monographs by H. Rachel, R. Bergmann and others in G. Schmoller, *Staats- und Sozialwissenschaftliche Forschungen* (Leipzig, 1878 ff., especially vols. 19 and 24).

As to the Great Elector's foreign policy, in addition to the *Urkunden und Aktenstücke* just mentioned, there are good accounts of his part in the First Northern War by E. Haumant, *La Guerre du Nord* (Paris, 1893); of his shifting alliances after 1660 by G. Pagès, *Le Grand Électeur et Louis XIV, 1660-1688* (Paris, 1905); and of his whole reign by A. Waddington, *Le Grand Électeur Frédéric Guillaume de Brandenbourg: sa Politique Extérieur, 1640-1688* (2 v., Paris, 1905-8).

The Great Elector's financial achievements, military innovations, and internal administration, briefly indicated in Riedel's *Staatshaushalt* and Jany's *Armee* mentioned above among the general works, are admirably detailed by K. Breysig and F. Wolters, *Geschichte der brandenburgischen Finanzen in der Zeit von 1640 bis 1697* (2 v., Munich and Leipzig, 1895-1915).

Readers interested in tactics and strategy may find satisfaction in T. A. Dodge, *Gustavus Adolphus: A History of the Art of War from its Revival after the Middle Ages to the End of the Spanish Succession War* (Boston, 1895).

For the history of Prussian administration in the eighteenth century the *Acta Borussica* are fundamental. They comprise several series. (1) *Die Behördenorganization* (ed. by G. Schmoller, O. Hintze *et al.*, 15 v., Berlin, 1894 ff., covering, as far as published, the years 1713 to 1772); this contains the documents, richly sprinkled with the pungent *marginalia* of Frederick William I and Frederick II, illustrating the development of the boards of government and the work of the General Directory. (2) *Getreidehandelspolitik* (ed. by G. Schmoller, G. Naudé and A. Skalweit, 3 v., 1896-1910) on the government's policy of restricting the importation and exportation of grain, and of buying it up and storing it in plentiful years when the price was low. (3) *Münzwesen* (ed. by F. Freiherr von Schrötter, 6 v., Berlin, 1904-11) on the coinage system. (4) *Seidenindustrie* (ed. by G. Schmoller and O. Hintze, 3 v., Berlin, 1892) on the silk industry. (5) *Wollenindustrie* (ed. by C. Hinrichs, Berlin, 1933) on the woolen industry under Frederick William I. To these should be added a work on the Hohenzollern zeal for settling colonists and improving agriculture, by R. Stadelmann, *Preussens Könige in ihrer Tätigkeit für die Landeskultur* (3 v., Leipzig, 1878-87).

Good general accounts of Germany, including Prussia, may be found in C. T. Atkinson, *History of Germany, 1713-1815* (London, 1908); *Cambridge Modern History,* VI, chs. 8, 9, 20, with bibliography; Sir R. Lodge, *Great Britain and Prussia in the Eighteenth Century* (Oxford, 1923); W. H. Bruford, *Germany in the Eighteenth Century* (Cambridge, Eng., 1935); K. S. Pinson, *Pietism as a Factor in the Rise of German Nationalism* (New York, 1934); and K. Francke, *History of German Literature or Social Forces in German Literature* (New York, 1897).

The best recent biography of Frederick William I is that

by F. von Oppeln-Bronikowski, *Der Baumeister des preussischen Staates* (Jena, 1934). His strained relations with his son, Fritz, and the latter's psychological development are excellently analyzed by the eminent French historian, E. Lavisse, *Youth of Frederick the Great* (London, 1891).

The standard biography of Frederick the Great is by the man who was long director of the Prussian archives, R. Koser, *König Friedrich der Grosse* (4 v., Stuttgart, 1912). Thomas Carlyle's *Frederick the Great* (6 v., London, 1858-65) is a masterpiece of English literature, good for Frederick's campaigns and battles, very inadequate on diplomatic, institutional and social history, and *sui generis* in style. The most interesting recent one-volume biography in German is G. Ritter, *Friedrich der Grosse: ein historisches Profil* (Leipzig, 1936), stimulating for its scholarship and for the parallels and lessons which it draws for contemporary Germany. Among the shorter accounts of the king in English are: W. F. Reddaway, *Frederick the Great and the Rise of Prussia* (New York, 1904); Norwood Young, *Life of Frederick the Great* (London, 1919); and F. J. P. Veale, *Frederick the Great* (London, 1935).

The best sources for the study of Frederick the Great, in addition to the *Acta Borussica* mentioned above, are his own voluminous writings, especially his *Politische Korrespondenz* (ed. by R. Koser, G. B. Volz *et al.*, 44 v., Berlin, 1879 ff.) comprising diplomatic, military, and miscellaneous despatches, sometimes in German and sometimes in French, and covering, as far as published, the period 1740-1780; and the *Oeuvres de Frédéric le Grand* (ed. by J. D. E. Preuss, 33 v., Berlin, 1846-57) comprising his literary writings: poems; correspondence with Voltaire, D'Argens, and other *philosophes;* histories of his ancestors, of his own times, and of the art of war; his attack on German literature; and a variety of other matters.

For the Silesian Wars, in addition to the good accounts in the biographies of Frederick mentioned above, recourse may be had to Prussian General Staff official history, *Die*

Kriege Friedrichs des Grossen (16 v., Berlin, 1890-1912), and to R. Waddington, *La Guerre de Sept Ans: Histoire diplomatique et militaire* (5 v., Paris, 1899-1914).

On the First Partition of Poland, see A. Sorel, *The Eastern Question in the Eighteenth Century* (London, 1898) for the European setting; R. H. Lord, *The Second Partition of Poland* (Cambridge, Mass., 1915, Introduction) for the weaknesses of Poland; Otto Hoetzsch, *Osteuropa und Deutscher Osten* (Berlin, 1934) for the contrast between Prussian and Polish institutional evolution; and for Frederick the Great's share in the partition, two articles by G. B. Volz in *Forschungen zur Brandb.-Preuss. Geschichte* (18:151-201 and 23:71-143, 224-5), and M. Bär, *West-preussen unter Friedrich dem Grossen* (2 v., Leipzig, 1909).

Harold Temperley, *Frederic the Great and Kaiser Joseph* (London, 1915), and Leopold von Ranke, *Die deutschen Mächte und der Fürstenbund* (Leipzig, 1875) give excellent accounts of Frederick II's efforts to hold in leash his restless Austrian neighbor.

Frederick's methods of work as an Enlightened Despot are very interestingly described in the penetrating study of W. L. Dorn, "The Prussian Bureaucracy in the Eighteenth Century" in the *Political Science Quarterly,* 46 : 403-423; 47 : 75-94, 259-273 (Sept., 1931-June, 1932). The best short book in English on this aspect of Frederick and his contemporaries is G. Bruun, *The Enlightened Despots* (New York, 1929).

Development of the Principal Organs

Dotted lines – – – – – – Organs of Brandenburg Electora[te]

1500	1600	1619	1640	1688

George William | **Frederick William, the Great Elector**

War or District Commissars — 1655 General Commissariat
Kriegs-Marsch- or Kreiskommissars — *Generalkommissariat*

1686
Marine
1682 Sta[...]
Ster[...]
1680 Comm[...]
Commer[...]

Bushel and Tolls Chest — 1674 Field War [...]
Metz-Lizentkasse — War Chest — *Feldkriegskasse*
Land-tax Chest — *Kriegskasse*
Kontributionskasse

1630·1641 War Council — Sparr — 1668 General Staff
Kriegsrat — *Generalstab*

Council — Privy Council
Rat — *Geheime Rat*

Elector in his Feudal Council

Administration and Foreign Affairs

1658 Judicial-Committee of the [...]
Justizrat

1651 State Finance Councillors — 16[...]
Staatskammerraete

Judicial | Ecclesiastical | Financial

Treasury (*Kammer*)

Comptroller's Office
Amtskammer

Privy Purse
Chatulle

Exchequer
Hofrentei

1673 Court State[...]
Hofstaatskasse

Postal Chest
Posthasse

1543 Consistory
Konsistorium

1540 Supreme Court
Kammergericht

Government in Brandenburg-Prussia

Solid lines————— General Organs of Prussian State

1713	1740	1786

erick III, (I as King) | Frederick William I | Frederick the Great

Chest

1722 Recruiting Chest
argenkasse
Rekrutenkasse
ax Chest
sse
Board
um

General War Chest
- - - - - - - - - - - - | *Generalkriegskasse*

Immediate Commissions

King in his Cabinet

General Directory: 4, later 9, Depts.
General-Ober-Finanz-Kriegs-und Domainen-Directorium

1698 State Conference for Foreign Affairs
Staatskonferenz or Cabinetsministerium

Council

1703 High Court of Appeal
Oberappellationsgericht

Comptroller's Office   1713 General Finance Directory
imo Hofkammer   *General-Finanz-Directorium*

1713 General Finance Chest
General-Finanz-Kasse or Domainenkasse

King's Chest
Dispositionskasse

1713 Brandenburg Exchequer
Landrentei

INDEX

(See also Hohenzollern Genealogy, facing p. 1, and Table of Organs of Government at end of volume.)

151

K

SUCH NICE KIDS

SUCH NICE KIDS

EVE BUNTING

Clarion Books
New York

Clarion Books
a Houghton Mifflin Company imprint
215 Park Avenue South, New York, NY 10003
Text copyright © 1990 by Eve Bunting

Library of Congress Cataloging-in-Publication Data
Bunting, Eve, 1928–
    Such nice kids / by Eve Bunting.
        p.   cm.
    Summary: When Jason allows a friend to borrow his mother's car
without her permission, one wrong move leads to another, escalating
into a tragedy.
    ISBN 0-395-54998-1
    I. Title.
PZ7.B91527   Stp   1990
[Fic]—dc20   90-30073
                                                              CIP
                                                              AC

BP 10 9 8 7 6 5 4 3 2 1

*For Jean Wickey and all my friends
in Bakersfield*

CHAPTER 1

What happened was my fault and Meeker's and Pidge's too. Though Meeker was mostly to blame. I wish I could stop going over it and over it, the way I do, trying to find excuses for myself, because there aren't any. Not for this.

• • •

I was locking my bike, about to head into Greenleaf's Gifts and Collectibles, when I heard Pidge calling my name and saw him lumbering toward me.

"Jase! Hey, Jase, wait up."

Oh, no! I thought. Pidge had been on a real downer ever since Elaine Masterson dumped him. Meeker and I told him "Good riddance" and "Forget her, she was raspy anyway." But nothing we said seemed to make Pidge feel any better. So I wasn't especially glad to see him, not when today was Destiny's birthday and I was on my way to buy her present and trying hard not to tell everybody I met: "Tonight I'm going out with Destiny Holbeck, the most beautiful girl in the world."

For a couple of seconds I thought about pretending I didn't hear Pidge and rushing on into the gift shop, hoping he wouldn't come after me. But he was only a few yards away. The good news was that he was beaming all over his face.

"Jase!"

"Hey, Pidgy, *you* look in a good mood."

"Yeah!" He ran his big hands through his blond stubble of hair. Meeker's always kidding Pidge, asking him when they let him out of San Quentin, or saying "My condolences, Pidge. I didn't know you got drafted." But Pidge has always had hair this short, ever since I can remember, even when all the other guys were wearing theirs long or in tails. His hair's the one thing Coach never has to get on him about.

"I met this girl," Pidge said, smiling his shy smile. "I asked her to go to Under 18 with me tonight and she said yes." Under 18 is a club in Santa Monica for teenagers that serves cool soft drinks and hot hard music. "I told her we were all going, having a party, and she said OK."

I thumped his shoulder. "Well, great, Pidge. Is she fine? Who is she?"

"She's fine, all right. She works at Radio Shack. I went in to get new batteries for my Walkman and we got talking. She and her mom just moved here from someplace in Illinois. So I asked her."

"Way to go!" I said.

Pidge was wearing his red letterman windbreaker with the big white *St. Jo's* on the front, St. Joseph's where he and Meeker and I would all be seniors, come September. I was wearing mine, too. June mornings in California are cool enough for a light jacket, but Pidge and I would probably still be wearing ours in the sizzle of August. St. Jo's football is big stuff here in Pasadena. And being varsity is really big stuff.

"So," Pidge said, "I'm all set. Except for one thing. Can we double up with you and Destiny?"

I rolled my eyes. "Aw, c'mon, Pidge, have a heart."

"But I got a *problem,* man. No wheels."

"What do you mean, no wheels?" I asked. "What's wrong with your mom's car? She lends it to you all the time."

Pidge did the massaging act on his hair again. "Mom and the girls are using the car. They're driving up to Aunt Meg's in San Bernardino. So, c'mon,

Jase." He gave me that look of his. I swear, I don't know how a guy can be six foot one and weigh 210 pounds and have a face like an angel. Coach is always telling him to sneer and scowl and look mean on the field.

"Pidge doesn't know how to look mean, Coach," we say, and it's true. Lucky he's the size he is.

"Natural intimidation," Meeker calls it. "Who wants to mess with a buffalo?"

"Look, maybe *she* has a car, the Radio Shack girl," I told Pidge.

"She doesn't."

I groaned. "For the last time, Pidge, I can't. Not tonight. And I've got to go now. It's Destiny's birthday and I've picked out something for her in here, in Greenleaf's."

Pidge jerked his head toward the donut shop next door. "Want a donut?"

I shook my head.

"Well, I'll get me a couple anyway and I'll wait for you. Take your time."

"Don't wait, Pidge," I said. "It's no use." But he would wait. I knew. What a pest, I thought. Pidge has always been a damn pest. Big old Pidge, who had braces on his legs when he was a kid, who was always hanging on me, who was always the last to be picked on the playground.

My mom liked to brag about how I was the only

one who ever chose him. "Jason would say: 'If Pidge doesn't play, I don't either.' And Jase was always so good they wanted *him*, so they had to take Pidge, too."

She doesn't tell anybody that anymore. I told her to quit it. I told her it was a put-down on Pidge, and that was all in the past. Pidge grew and grew, bigger than anybody, and now he was a football star, and all-league, and he didn't need to be pitied. And anyway, I didn't pick Pidge because I was some sort of saint. I picked him because he was my best friend and that didn't change, however hard that was for everybody to understand.

Once I'd come into our kitchen where my mom and Meeker's mom were sitting at the table, drinking coffee, and Meeker's mom was saying, "It's so strange the way the three of them hang out together!" She was talking about Meeker and Pidge and me. "I mean, Pidge isn't exactly *retarded*, but he's so slow thinking. By rights he should drive them mad. And as for that house he lives in . . ."

Mom had interrupted in her quiet, even voice. "Pidge is a really nice kid."

Right on, Mom. My mom is OK.

Through the plate-glass window of the donut shop I could see the really nice kid paying for his jelly-filled and chocolate-sprinkled. He'll wait, all right, I thought. He always waits. I pushed open the door of the gift shop, hearing the small warning bell chime softly.

"Hi!" The woman behind the counter looked up and smiled. She was the one who'd taken my deposit last week and who'd put Destiny's gift away for me. I thought she was probably about my grandma's age, but much more with it.

"I've come to pay the rest," I said. "Last week I gave you . . ."

"I know. I'll go get the rose."

I got out my wallet and took forty bucks from it, my total tips from three nights parking cars at the April Gardens restaurant.

Now the lady was back, carrying a long skinny box in both hands. "I wrapped it already but I didn't put the ribbon on in case you wanted another look."

"Yes, please," I said.

She laid the box gently on the counter, lifted the lid and the folded layers of tissue on top. Underneath, cradled in more paper, was the crystal rose.

"I'd forgotten how pretty it is," I said staring down at it. In the box the rose was the clear pure color of ice water but when I leaned over, it reflected my jacket, turning a deep, dark red that shaded to pink along the narrow stem.

I took it out, very carefully, and saw the blue of the saleslady's dress in its glass depths and a flash of brightness like sunlight. That was the reflection of a yellow china cat on the shelf behind.

"It's gorgeous, all right," the lady said.

She laid the rose in the box again and we squared away the money part. Then she asked, "What color ribbon? We have white, yellow, or red."

I thought of Destiny. "Red, please."

She cut off a piece of ribbon long enough for a jump rope and spread it across the box.

"I expect this is for your girl, right?"

"Well . . ." I could have said "Don't I wish" or "I'm hoping," but I settled on "Yes."

"Lucky girl." The lady's fingers manipulated the bow. "What's her name?"

"Destiny." Even saying it gave me pleasure.

She flashed me a smile. "So you have a date with destiny?"

"Something like that." I tried to look as if this was a real original remark instead of one I'd heard a dozen times. I'd heard all the destiny jokes possible, including one from my dad.

"Destiny rides again," he'd said.

"That's supposed to be Destry, not Destiny," my mom told him.

The saleslady stood back to admire her work.

"It looks great," I said. "Thanks." I hooked my backpack over my arm, picked up the box, and held it carefully away from me as I walked.

"It's not *that* fragile," she called after me. "Just hold it gently but firmly, you know, the way you hold Destiny."

I felt my face getting hot. Don't I wish, I thought again. And then I thought, Maybe tonight. Tonight is going to be super special.

Pidge was still waiting outside, of course, leaning against the video store window, eating the jelly donut. He'd brought his bike over and propped it in the rack beside mine.

"Hold this," I told him. "And be careful. I have to unlock my bike. Don't drop it, Pidge, and don't get jelly on it."

He stuffed the rest of the donut in his mouth, wiped his hands on his jeans, and took the gift.

I walked my bike one-handed, with the box cradled safely under my arm, and he walked beside me.

"Meeker told me you're taking Destiny out to dinner first," Pidge said.

"Yep."

"I wouldn't expect us to go to dinner with you, Jase," he went on. "Me and my new girl, I mean. I don't have the bucks. It's just, you know, afterward, to the club."

"Ask Meeker, why don't you?" I said. "Meeker's the one who organized the Under 18 thing in the first place."

"His car only takes two. You know that, Jase."

"Yeah, but maybe he knows somebody who's going and has room. Lucian or Bellman . . ."

"They wouldn't want me."

"Sure they would," I said heartily, knowing Pidge was probably right.

The jacaranda trees were in bloom, dropping their flowers like blue snowflakes on the sidewalk; they crunched as we walked through them. I wished Pidge wouldn't keep putting me in this sort of bind. I wished he'd just go home, but he was still with me as we turned onto Oakdale, where I live.

My mom and dad had left this morning for a week in San Francisco. Dad had a five-day CPA conference and Mom took time off from work to go with him. The double garage doors were down and already our house had that empty look that would probably make it real attractive to every burglar in town. I'd taken the *Times* in before I left this morning, but the mailbox bulged and my *Sports Illustrated* and Dad's *Kiplinger Report* lay on the mat by the front door, another green flag for burglars.

I stopped by the bottom step. "Pidge. You can come in if you want, but I swear, you are *not* coming with Destiny and me tonight. Look, I've been planning this for weeks. We'd have to go all the way to Santa Monica for dinner . . . I told you I made the reservations at the Haven . . . and then come back and get you and the — you know, the Radio Shack girl. And besides, it's my first chance to be alone with Destiny, really alone, and I honestly don't want to risk . . ."

"Well, then I can't go, that's all. And Elaine's going to be there with Beamish."

"Elaine Masterson with John Beamish? But he's such a jerk."

"The girls don't think so," Pidge said. "I wanted Elaine to see that I could get another girl, a really cute girl — that she's not the only one . . ."

I interrupted. "You could get a *dozen* girls, Pidge. What are you talking about?"

"No I couldn't, Jase. I still don't know how I got Elaine."

"It's because he's on the team," Meeker had said. "That's the only reason Elaine Masterson even gave Pidge a second look. If he got dumped she'd drop him so fast he'd squish."

Pidge hadn't been dropped from the team. But school was out, it was summer, the glory season was over, and the next one hadn't started. I hated myself for the way that thought flashed into my head, and for remembering how Elaine had been on the beach last summer, apologizing for Pidgy all the time. She'd draped a towel over him and laughed. "Cover up, fat boy." Pidge had laughed too and clowned around, pretending the towel was a tent, but I remembered the way his lips quivered when he thought no one was looking.

I sighed. "Come on in, Pidge. We'll call Meek and ask his advice."

Pidge grinned. "Yeah! Meek'll know what to do."

If only I hadn't suggested that, because that was the beginning, right then. That was the first fatal step. But I did suggest it.

"Do you think Meek'll be home yet?" Pidge asked.

"We can call and see."

Meeker lives just across the street from me, but his driveway is so long and so hidden by trees that you can't tell if his little Sting Ray is there or not. The Corvette was a sixteenth birthday present from his folks. Pretty nice.

"You go ahead and call." I nodded down at the gift box. "I want to take this upstairs."

"You mean you're not going to show me what you got for her? Come on, Jase."

"Nah." I touched the ribbon. "I don't want to ruin it."

"You could slide it off. I'd like to see it, Jason."

I hesitated, wanting to show it, wanting Pidgy to admire it, wanting another look at it myself.

"Well, OK." Carefully I skimmed the ribbon to the edge of the box and over the side. I lifted the lid and the folds of tissue paper and there was the crystal rose, red again as it reflected us, so perfect, so pure.

"Wow! Can I touch it?" Pidge breathed.

"Yeah. But don't lift it. And if you break it I'll break your neck."

He ran his big, clumsy fingers over the petals, not saying anything.

"Well?" I asked.

"It's so pretty. Like a sunset." He looked at me with his big blue eyes. "I wish I had one just like it. Maybe I could save . . ."

"You'd never make it," I told him. "This thing cost major bucks." And I was thinking how Pidgy had a birthday coming up and how Meeker and I could maybe split the cost of one of these roses. We might have to special order it. Meeker would laugh his head off, but maybe I could talk him into not telling anybody, just keeping his mouth shut and doing it. Pidge would be stoked. I'd almost forgotten how much he loved pretty things.

I slid the lid back on and eased the ribbon in place. "Good as new. If you want to talk to Meek, go ahead and call. I'll take this upstairs."

I heard Pidge on the phone as I set the box on my dresser. The digital clock by the bed said 2:20. I'd be picking Destiny up in just about three hours. I looked at myself in the mirror, my straight dark hair, pale skin, pale eyes. "Celtic," my mother always said. "Irish from way back."

I thought of Destiny. Olive skin, dark serious eyes, long hair that hung black as my own down her back or swung high in a thick braid. "A date with Destiny," I said to my reflection in the mirror, and I felt this quaking nervousness inside that doesn't come when I think of any other girl.

"Hey, Jase!" Pidge called from the bottom of the stairs. "Meek's there. He's on his way over. He says no sweat, he's got everything figured out for me already."

"He would," I said and smiled. It seemed like such a little thing, getting Pidge a ride to the club. That's the way it seemed, then.

CHAPTER 2

I came running down the stairs when the doorbell rang. Pidge had already let Meeker in. He was standing in the hallway, dark and stocky.

"Hi, Meek," I said.

"How you doin', Jase?" He unzipped his leather bomber jacket, threw it on the couch, threw himself down beside it. "I hear we have a problem."

"Somewhat," I said. "But I hear you've got it wired."

Pidge sat on the edge of the couch next to Meeker, his hands clasped between his knees, toes turned in as usual. Pidge has three younger sisters and they're *all* pigeon-toed, same as he is. They all had leg braces, too. The braces didn't help any, as far as I could tell, but then as my mom says, they could have been worse without them. Pidge's real name is Bill. I don't know who first began calling him Pidge, but I know I knocked a girl down in first grade for calling him that. Then Pidge started calling himself Pidge. That's how his name reads on the football roster . . . Pidge Glovsky, Linebacker.

"So how do I get me and my date to the dance, Meek?" he asked.

"There are two cars in Jason's garage, aren't there?" Meeker asked. "His mom's and his dad's. He uses one and you use the other."

I snorted. "Are you serious? No way."

Meeker raised his eyebrows. "You're using two yourself, Jase?"

"No. I'm taking my dad's."

"So? What's the problem? Pidge can take your mom's."

Pidge's head was turning from one of us to the other as we talked. His smile came and went.

"My mom's stays where it is." Anger rose inside of me. Typical Meeker. He's always doing things like this, putting someone else on the spot.

"What about *you* lending Pidge Babs's car? Or Harry's?" I asked him. Babs and Harry are Meeker's parents. "Just call me Babs," Mrs. Meeker tells all the kids, tossing her streaky blond hair and flashing her long, tanned legs. For some reason Babs always seems to be in white shorts, heading for the tennis club or coming home from it.

"Babs and Harry don't lend their cars, you know that," Meeker said. "That's why they bought me one of my own."

"Hey, Jase, I bet your mom wouldn't mind," Pidge said, standing up.

I gritted my teeth and tried to make my voice casual. "Do you want a diet ginger ale, Pidge? Meeker?"

"Yeah, sure."

I swung around and headed for the kitchen. Behind me I heard Meeker asking Pidge about his new date and about what time they planned on getting to Under 18, as if it were all settled.

Sure, I thought, grabbing three soft-drink cans from the refrigerator and banging them on the counter, then rooting in the pantry cupboard for the bag of pretzels. I skimmed the bag so hard across the counter that it fell on the floor.

Meeker says it, and so it happens. Well, not this time. "I never can figure out why you and Meeker are such great friends," my dad says. He's said it more than once. "You're not the same kind of boys at all."

He's right about that.

"It's because they've always known each other,"

Mom says. "Since before they were born, even." My mom and Meek's were pregnant at the same time. "And besides, when they were little they were the only two boys on the street," she adds. "They had to play together. It got to be a habit."

A habit I got sick of sometimes. Like now.

I stuffed a can of ginger ale in each pocket, carried the other one, the pretzels, and three bananas into the living room.

"Let's just keep cool heads about this car business," Meeker said. He popped a can, sticking his finger into the froth that bubbled up, sucking at it.

"One, the car's there and nobody's using it," Meeker pointed out. "Two, our very good friend Pidge needs a car for a very good reason, and I don't have room in the Corvette."

Meeker took a quick swig of ginger ale. "Three, Pidge is an excellent driver without even a ticket to his name. He's so good he was recommended by his friend, Jason Flynn, to be his partner parking cars weekends at April Gardens, one of our top local restaurants, and is therefore used to handling Rolls-Royces, Jaguars . . .

I interrupted him. "I can't lend him Mom's car without her say-so."

"So call and get her say-so."

Pidge beamed. "Yeah."

I held up my hands. "OK, OK." I'd let Mom tell Pidge "No" herself. That would finish it.

But when the hotel switchboard rang my parents' room, there was no answer. There was no answer when we called a half hour and another ginger ale later. I could have left a message but I didn't.

"Nobody goes to San Francisco to hang around a hotel," I said. "They're out taking a cable car ride or something." And when they came back it would be too late.

Pidge slumped on the couch.

I looked at him and I thought, Shoot, here I go again. I'm not going to give him Mom's car so I'll have to let him and this girl ride with me and Destiny. There's no other solution.

I'd made dinner reservations for Destiny and me at the Haven in Santa Monica so we could go straight from there to Under 18. And I'd pictured maybe a walk on the beach first, with the dark coming down and the waves rippling across the sand and over our bare feet. The Haven wasn't right on the beach, we'd have to drive over and park, but still.

I'd tried for Scottie's first because Scottie's was prime, built on pilings with the ocean swirling below it. But trying to get reservations at Scottie's is like trying to get on the space shuttle to the moon. The Haven was second best. Now we weren't even going to have second best. I'd have to try for something ordinary and local.

For a minute I felt like shaking Pidge. Why couldn't he handle things for himself? And Meeker, why did he always have to butt in? I looked at him lounging on the couch, his feet propped on the coffee table, his fingers laced behind his head.

"Hey, Jase? Did you get those reservations you wanted at Scottie's?" Meeker didn't even open his eyes.

"No." I felt like telling him to mind his own stupid business.

"Well, you have them now," Meeker said. "You've got a window table for two, my friend. Seven o'clock."

"You're kidding."

"My dad called for you. He knows Scottie." Meeker's eyes opened and for a second our glances held before he looked away.

"That was real nice of him," I said.

"Wow!" Pidge said. "Your dad knows *Scottie?* Your dad knows everybody, Meek."

"Yeah, well, that's how Harry is."

I know how he is. Meeker and I share an understanding of his dad. Sometimes I think that's been one of the big bonds between us, not the stuff Mom talks about. That and the fact that I don't talk about

| 19

what I know about Harry. Not even to Meeker. Meeker just knows I know.

"Tell him thanks," I said.

"So now we've got you taken care of and we just need to concentrate on Pidge's plight." Meeker grinned. "I like that. 'Pidge's plight.' It's like the title of a movie."

I opened my mouth to say I'd made a decision and Pidge could ride with Destiny and me. But then I remembered Scottie's, and that Destiny and I were going there now, thanks to Meeker's dad. So I was right back where I'd started; I'd have to drive all the way to Santa Monica and back again for Pidge and his date. That was crazy. Besides, there'd be no time.

"Aw, just let him use your mom's car, why don't you," Meeker said. "It's no big deal. You can tell your parents you tried to call for permission. Anyway, your mom will never know. Pidge, you put gas in that car and leave it just the way you got it. No old beer cans on the floor or cigarette butts in the ashtray."

Pidge, neither a drinker nor a smoker, didn't even smile. He just sat shaking his head.

"Naw. You don't have to lend it to me, Jase. I know you don't want to."

I looked at Pidge and had one of my drawbacks. That's what I call it when I'm drawn back to something that happened with Pidge and me when we were little. They're drawbacks for me, all right, because they make me so sorry for him that I fold right up the middle.

At this minute, I was remembering the time a bunch of us were going hiking up Cheney Trail. It must have been the summer after fifth grade. Pidge still had his leg braces, and everybody had been careful not to mention the hike when he was around in case he'd want to go. I'd been quieter than anybody. And then he'd come clomping into our kitchen just when we were all there, our water bottles filled, our lunches packed, our hiking boots mink-oiled and ready. Meeker wasn't there; I can't remember why now. I think he was in Europe or somewhere with his parents.

"Can I go?" Pidge had asked, eyes shining, and there'd been this awful, embarrassed silence.

I remembered the guilt I'd felt because I hadn't told him, hadn't included my best friend. It was probably the guilt that spoke for me. "Sure you can," I'd said, too loudly, and there'd been all this shuffling around me, and Tommy O'Neil, I remember it was Tommy O'Neil, coughed a little warning cough. I'd added: "If you think you can keep up," and let my voice drag away at the end.

"You don't have to take me, Jase. It's OK." Pidge had slouched there, rubbing one brace against the other, shaking his big head just the way he was shaking it now.

I swear, I hate these drawbacks. I wish I could erase them like marks on a chalkboard.

I sighed. "I guess it'll be OK if you take Mom's car," I said. "That's the easiest thing for everyone."

"You mean it?" Pidge was smiling all over his face. "You think it'll be all right with your mom?"

"I don't know. But we're telling her right after she gets back. You and me together, Pidge. OK?"

"OK. Great. No problem." Pidge rubbed his hands together. "Gee, thanks a lot, Jase."

Meeker tipped the last of the pretzels from the package into his mouth and scooped up his leather jacket. "OK, then we're set. It's going to be dyno."

He stood and stretched so his muscles bulged. Every day of his life Meeker works out with weights. He doesn't play ball, though. He could. Way back in Little League baseball and Junior Football days, Meeker started every season, but he never finished. Meeker gets bored real easy.

"Can I take the car now?" Pidge asked me.

I stood, uncertain. "Let me try to get Mom one more time."

Meeker rolled his eyes. "It's not as if you're lending him a *Porsche*, for Pete's sake. It's just a Ford Fairlane, and an old one at that."

"Yeah, well, it's my mother's old Ford and it's the

only one she's got," I said. "I swear, Meek, you're such a pain in the butt."

There was still no answer from my parents' room, but this time I asked the hotel operator to leave them a message to call me.

I wasn't feeling good about what I'd done. The drawback had temporarily vanished and I was left thinking how stupid I'd been to agree to something like this. Right then I should have said, "Look, I've changed my mind, Pidge. You can't have the car." But I didn't.

"So will I take it now?" Pidge asked again.

"I'll be leaving pretty soon to pick up Destiny," I said. "I'll give you Mom's keys and one of the garage openers. You can come back for the car later." And I thought, The less time he has it the better.

"*Oooo!* He's going to be leaving soon to pick up *Destiny,*" Meeker told Pidge. "Too cool!"

Pidge grinned.

As if on a signal, he and Meeker put their heads together and began to sing an old-time song called "My Fate, My Destiny." Meeker had found the sheet music in some moldy old bookstore and given it to me. On the front was a picture of a guy with black licorice hair parted in the middle. I had it pinned up in my room. "He looks like Dracula," Meeker had said. "I'd keep a clove of garlic under my pillow if I were you."

"My fate, my destiny..." Pidge and Meeker warbled.

"Cut it out, you guys," I said, feeling this heat all over me. "I'll get the keys."

"So we'll see you and your Destiny at about nine," Meeker said. "After you've dined and ..." He rolled his eyes.

"She's not *my* Destiny," I said but Meeker paid no attention.

"It'll be smooth," he said. "Pidge and ... what's her name, Pidge?"

"Valerie."

"You and Destiny, Pidge and Valerie, me and Zoe."

"And everybody else, of course," I added.

Pidge's hand shot out for the keys. "Hey, Jase. Thanks a lot. I'll take good care of the car. You don't have to worry."

"You better, bozo. And what do you mean I don't have to worry? I'll worry."

I watched them cross the street. Pidge big and loose and shapeless in his red windbreaker, pushing his bike, Meek neat and cocky, his bomber jacket slung like a bullfighter's cape over his shoulder. Once Zoe, Meeker's girl, had said to me, "Don't you think it's funny that his name is Meek? I mean, you think 'meek' and you for sure don't think someone like *him*. He should be called 'Bold' or 'Brave.'"

"Give me a break, Zoe," I'd begged. But she wasn't far wrong.

The magnolia trees were in bloom and the day was filled with their sweet lemony smell. A shiver of a breeze shook some petals down to lie on the grass.

I was shivery myself suddenly as I closed the door and went inside to get ready for my date with Destiny.

CHAPTER 3

Almost the first thing I did after Pidge and Meeker left was call Scottie's and make sure about the dinner reservations. When Meeker's dad makes the arrangements, you can't take anything for granted. In fact, it's smart not to believe half of what he says.

A woman answered the phone and I could tell she was young. "Yes sir, we have you down for seven P.M. A window table." She paused. "Didn't you call to check on these about an hour ago?"

"No," I said.

"I could have sworn! I think somebody did. Well, you're all set."

"Thanks." I hung up and I thought, Meeker called in too, because he wasn't sure about his dad's arrangements, either.

There was no need to get dressed up for Scottie's or Under 18. I wouldn't need a jacket for either. "Just simple understated trendiness," I told myself, grinning at my reflection that showed my khaki-colored shirt with its trademark red button and the white pants that Mom had bought for me at Buffums' sale.

"What are those? Pirate pantaloons?" Dad had asked.

"Those are high fashion, my dear," Mom told him.

I looked at myself and said out loud, "A little confidence to go with the high fashion would be nice, Jason." But for me, the thought of Destiny and self-confidence didn't go together.

It was too early to leave. Bad to be on her doorstep ahead of time, all sweaty and anxious. I ate a banana to hold me till seven P.M. dinner, brushed my teeth again, and took another swig of Scope. My tongue felt numb. Maybe I'd overdone the mouthwash.

When the phone rang I had this horrible, bottomed-out feeling that it was Destiny and she'd changed her mind about going out with me.

It was Dad. "Hi, Jason. Are you OK?"

"Fine. I tried to call you earlier."

"I know. We got your message. Is everything all right?"

I paused. "Fine." Should I get into the car business with Dad? Dad wasn't as easygoing as Mom.

"Tonight's the night you have the party at the Santa Monica club, right?" he asked.

"Right."

"Well, drive carefully. The Dodgers are in New York so there shouldn't be too much traffic on the freeway. But be careful. And have a good time."

"I will. Thanks." I watched a small spider drop from the ceiling on an invisible thread and hang motionless in front of my face. I *had* to ask about the car. I just had to. But suppose Dad said no?

The spider swung as if on a trapeze.

If Dad said no, how would I tell Pidge? He was all jazzed up. I'd given him the keys already.

"Could I speak to Mom for a minute?" I asked.

"She's not here. She stopped in the gift shop in the lobby and I came on up and found your message."

"Oh. OK."

"Do you want her to call you back?"

"Naw. I'll be leaving in a couple of minutes. It's not important. Just calling to check that you're having a good time."

"We are, and we'll call again tomorrow, Jase. Have fun."

"You too, Dad. Good night."

I hung up the phone and stood looking at it.

Dad's strict about stuff. Not mean, but strict. I'd lay a bet he'd have said no to the car. It was a good thing I hadn't asked.

I touched the spider with my finger and he went up the thread as fast as a ray of light and disappeared.

. . .

It was a clear, beautiful evening.

Sprinklers seesawed in front yards leaving trails of rainbows. On Ridgemore Road, where Destiny lives, kids played softball on the street and older people sat on front steps. It was so different from our neighborhood where you never see anyone except gardeners at work. This was friendlier somehow, more homey.

The box that held the crystal rose lay on the back seat of Dad's car covered with my St. Jo's jacket. I wondered when I should give it to her. If I'd brought a *real* flower, now would have been the time, right at the beginning of our date. But with the crystal rose I wasn't so sure.

I stopped at the curb in front of her house and checked in the driver's mirror to make sure my cowlick hadn't popped up at the back of my hair. I swear, that cowlick is like a barometer. If I get nervous or excited, up it springs out of nowhere. It had misfired this time though, because I was both nervous and excited and it still lay flat on top. Good. I examined my tongue in the mirror, too. It looked OK and it had stopped being numb.

It was Destiny who opened the door when I rang the bell.

"Hi."

"Hi."

Her smile brought out the dimple at the corner of her mouth. Sometimes, in English Lit, which is the only class we have together, Mr. Colombo says something funny and I turn to check if Destiny's smiling. I pretend I'm not looking at her. I pretend I'm staring past her at Pidge who sits two rows over. That dimple really does me in.

"I'm not late, am I?" I asked.

"Uh-uh. Perfect timing."

She was wearing a white miniskirt with white sandals and a bright yellow shirt. Her hair was in its high-strutting black braid and there was a crumple of orange and yellow ribbons, or maybe flowers, holding it on top. She just about took my breath away.

Meeker couldn't figure why I was so besotted with Destiny. "Besotted" was his word, not mine.

"She's OK looking," he said. "But not great, like Zoe or Cassie Walker."

I agreed. She wasn't like Zoe or Cassie Walker. Or anybody else. That's probably why I was besotted.

"You look nice," I told her now.

"Thanks. You too."

"It's not that she's *heavy*," Meeker says. "But she's not exactly — slender. Sturdy maybe. What do you think, Pidge? Would sturdy be the word for Destiny?"

"To me she looks strong, like an Indian princess," Pidge says, and I think Yes, Pidge, that is perfect. He could have added that she's the color an Indian princess might be, too, olive-skinned and smooth. And that she has great long, tanned legs.

I smoothed my hair to check my cowlick again and make sure the sight of her legs in that miniskirt hadn't excited it. But it was still OK.

"Destiny Holbeck would be too quiet for me," Meeker says.

She would be. Meeker can't stand quiet. And then, because he's shrewd and smart, he gives me a look and adds, "That's why old Jase is obsessed with her. He thinks she's dark and filled with secrets, like her name."

Maybe that *is* why I'm obsessed. Partly. Meeker knows me pretty well.

Destiny walked ahead of me now down the path, black braid swaying. An Indian princess, I thought, and I remembered back to the fourth grade when we read about Pocahontas who held the head of John Smith in her arms as he was about to be killed.

I opened the car door.

"We're going to Scottie's instead of the Haven," I told her. "Meeker's dad fixed it."

"Scottie's? Great!" She smiled and the dimple appeared.

"And then we'll meet the others at Under 18. They'll be there at eight but I told them we'd be later, around nine. OK?"

"Perfect," she said.

I had the car radio on, tuned to "The Wave," and we didn't talk a lot on the way to Santa Monica. But there was nothing uncomfortable in the silence. We rapped a bit about school and about a movie we'd both seen, though not together. I wondered if she'd been with another girl, or another guy. I knew a few things about her. Her parents were divorced and she lived with her mom and her younger sister, Aurora, who'd be starting St. Jo's next year.

"My mother's name is just plain Mary Jane," she told me now. "I guess that's how come we got to be Destiny and Aurora. If I ever have a daughter she'll be nice, sensible Mary Jane."

I gathered in every word, hungry for information about her. Maybe that's how it is when you're obsessed.

My dad had been right about the traffic. There wasn't much. But then, just past the Fairfax off-ramp, we began slowing, and way ahead of the line of cars I could see flashing red lights.

"Oh, no, an accident," I said.

We crawled along, me keeping an anxious eye on my watch. A window table at Scottie's was at risk here.

But we were moving faster now and I figured a tow truck had cleared the lane. There it was, hooked onto a blue Toyota van with a smashed-in side. Three police cars were in the emergency lane, too, and an ambulance and a fire truck. Orange flares still flickered, burned almost to stubs. And then I saw the white car, squashed like a bug against the center divider.

"How awful," Destiny said. "The van must have sideswiped it."

I didn't even look at the van. The car was a white Ford. Mom's? Pidge? But how could he have gotten here ahead of us? I felt sick; was it a Ford? No, it was a Chevrolet. *Of course* it wasn't Pidge.

I swallowed and slowed some more. A police officer waved me impatiently on, mouthing, "Keep moving. Keep moving."

I eased my grip on the wheel. How stupid. There must be a million white cars in California. What an idiot I'd been to freak out like that!

We were speeding up again now, driving through the tunnel into Santa Monica with its first magical unfolding of sand and shimmering sea. Usually I get a high right here, especially at this time of evening when the sun's just about to set, laying a red path across the ocean. There's always a flurry of last sailboats tacking through it, hurrying back to harbor.

Tonight with Destiny beside me the magic was stronger than ever. Except that the memory of the freeway accident came back to chill me. It came back, too, at odd moments during dinner. That and my dad's voice asking, "Is everything all right?" Sure, Dad. Everything's great. Nothing to worry about.

Once I looked at my watch. It was seven-thirty and I thought, Pidge is picking up Valerie just about now. And at eight I thought, They'll be at Under 18. All is well. Fine. Nothing to worry about.

The meal had been wonderful. We'd had shrimp cocktail, salmon poached in some sort of mellow sauce, baby potatoes. It was just the way I'd imagined it — the red sunset sky, lights turning the waves to a rumble-tumble of silver, Destiny across the little table from me.

There was a piano player with a low, gravelly voice who sang old romantic songs, like "Stardust" and "That Old Black Magic." He was perfect, too. Destiny and I were just making a decision about dessert when he leaned close to his microphone and purred, "Now I have a special request for Jason and . . ." He paused and cat-smiled under his mustache. "For Jason and his Destiny, who are with us this evening."

"Oh, no," I whispered.

"My fate, my destiny," he sang.

"Look cool," I whispered to Destiny. "Pretend we aren't the ones." I stared around as if scanning the room.

"*You* requested this?" Destiny whispered.

"Uh-uh. Meeker must have called it in. I think I'm going to kill that guy."

We applauded politely at the end with everyone else.

"Whew," I said. "Let's have double desserts. We deserve them."

"I loved the song," Destiny said. "But I'll have a double dessert anyway."

We had a small, friendly debate over the check. "This place is so expensive," Destiny said.

I cut her off. "Forget it. My grandma is very generous. She sends a check on Labor Day, Memorial Day, Arbor Day, United Nations Day. Besides, this is for your birthday."

"And how did you find out about that?" she asked.

"I have my ways." And there's still the crystal rose, I thought. I'll give her that at the door when I leave her tonight. I'll put it in her arms and I'll say "Happy Birthday" and maybe I'll kiss her. I hadn't yet. Third date and I hadn't even kissed her. Meeker would die laughing. Of course the other two times we'd been with a group so it wasn't the same. Maybe tonight I'd hold her gently but firmly, the way the saleslady said.

When the valet brought Dad's car around I gave him two bucks. What the heck! I was in a great mood, and if I was spending Grandma's money this freely I might as well be generous to a fellow parking attendant.

"Thank you, sir," he said.

It sure was nice to be on the other side of the social fence for once.

I rolled down the car windows as we drove back along the Coast Highway. The smell of the ocean, salty and fishy, drifted into the car and already we could hear the pulse of the music drifting across from the pier.

"'Stardust' it isn't," I told Destiny. We smiled at each other and I was thinking, There isn't anywhere in the world as warm and close as the inside of a car, with the dark outside and someone special beside you.

The music was getting louder now. I could already tell there'd be no parking left on the pier so we cruised the lot by the beach, searching for a space. We found the last one in the farthest corner. I knew I'd been halfway searching for something else, too, as we drove around. There was Meeker's car. But where was Mom's? Not seeing it made me nervous again, which was crazy. There were other parking lots. Pidge might have been here early enough to find pier space.

I hoped he'd locked up carefully. I hoped he'd left the car where there was good lighting. Sure he had. Pidge wasn't stupid. Relax, I told myself. Cut out this paranoid stuff.

We walked across the sand and up the steps to the rickety, wonderful old pier. It was jammed with people, families with kids, middle-aged couples. The carousel's tinny music competed with the bang and clatter of the bumper cars, the sudden sharp cracks from the rifle range. Up at the pier's end, jutting out into the swell of the ocean, was Under 18, its neon sign flashing red and green and purple, music blasting from it. Kids milled about, hanging over the railing to look at the ocean, huddling in the shadows to kiss. I saw Elaine Masterson, Pidge's ex-girlfriend, with John Beamish, her new boy-friend.

"Jason! Jason, over here!"

I pointed. "There's Meeker," I said.

We edged in his direction.

He had Zoe in tow, tottering on high heels. She

was wearing a tight black dress with white spots on it and some kind of lighted band flashed on and off in her frizz of dark hair.

Meeker put his face close to mine. "Have you seen Pidge?"

My heart began a slow, heavy beat.

"No. Isn't he here yet? What time is it?"

I held up my wrist to look at my watch and Zoe bent her head with its flickering headband so I'd have more light. "It's ten past nine," I said.

"Wasn't he supposed to be here at eight?" Destiny asked me.

I nodded. "That's what he said."

Meeker and I stood looking at each other, letting the noise surround us.

Pidge wasn't here. He'd taken off in the borrowed car — my mom's borrowed car — and he'd never arrived. I think somewhere deep inside I'd been expecting this.

CHAPTER 4

"You're positive he's not here?" I asked Meek, shouting so he could hear me over the noise.

"Positive."

"Well, do we have to keep waiting around for *all* your buddies to arrive, Meeker?" Zoe yelled. "One of them's here now." The heel of her sandal had stuck between two of the boards of the pier and she bent to pull it out. For the first time I noticed that the lights on her hair band spelled out LOOK AT ME. Who could help it?

"Let's go inside and have some fun," she urged.

"In a minute," Meeker said.

I pointed to the steps and the beach below. "Down there. We could hear ourselves think."

Zoe pulled off her shoes as soon as we got on the sand.

"I don't understand why you're so worried about Pidge," Destiny said. "Couldn't he have just changed his mind about coming?"

The lights from the pier threw our shapes on the pale sand and I nudged the shadow of her braid with my foot.

"He wouldn't change his mind about this," I said.

Zoe printed her name on the sand with her bare toe. "He probably just got stuck in traffic," she said impatiently. "Let's go back to the party." She spread her arms wide and twirled so that her headband words became ribbons of light. "If he comes, he comes."

Meeker looked at me. "Could have been an accident."

"We'll give him till ten," I said. "If he isn't here by then, we'd better go looking."

Meeker and Destiny and I stayed close to the doors so we'd spot Pidge when he came, but Zoe disappeared into the crowd with a bunch of other St. Joers. After a while the three of us found a table near the entrance and got root beers from the bar.

At ten Pidge still hadn't appeared. Destiny went to the ladies' room and while she was gone I said to Meeker, "Maybe he decided not to put me in a spot after all by taking Mom's car."

"Naw. He'd have called to tell me. Or he'd have called you at Scottie's."

Destiny was pushing back toward us now through the crowd and I couldn't believe how, even in the middle of this, the sight of her made my heart lift. I asked her if she'd mind if we left now.

She shook her head. "Not a bit."

"You two wait in front," Meeker said. "I'll get Zoe."

But he came out without her. "She wants to stay. She says somebody'll bring her home. Let's go."

Well, I thought. Even for Meeker abandoning your date seemed a bit much. But that was Meeker. And I guess that was Zoe, too.

We walked away from Under 18, the sea air clean and cold and zippy after the crowded, noisy club.

"You don't have a sweater?" I asked Destiny.

"No. But I'm OK."

We were walking faster now and I thought it was nice the way Destiny strode long-legged between us, not chattering or making a fuss about leaving. I decided it was no wonder I was obsessed with her.

"The first thing we should do is try calling Pidge," I told Meeker. "If he's at home, we can all stop sweating."

Between us we found the right change and I called from the phone booth where the pier ended and the boardwalk began. There was no answer, just the ringing on the other end mixed with the tinny music of the carousel and the steady *thump thump* from the club.

"Meek? You didn't hear him say Valerie's last name, did you?" I asked.

"No. but you could try Radio Shack. If somebody's there they might give you her number."

"I doubt it. Anyhow, it'll be closed."

It was. All I got was a recording giving their hours of business.

We sat down on one of the benches, staring out across the ocean.

"So now what?" I asked and answered my own question. "I guess we should head for Pasadena. If we don't find him stranded somewhere along the freeway, Meek, I'll take Destiny home and we'll meet at my house. OK?"

"OK. But if we do find him on the freeway . . . ?" Meeker let the question hang.

I bit my lip. "Then take the first off-ramp and double back behind him. We will, too."

"Right," Meeker said.

• • •

I drove in the fast lane so we could see more easily across the divider. Ahead of us, Meeker's four round taillights gleamed red as fire, the car so low-slung we couldn't even see the top of his head.

"What does Pidge's mom's car look like?" Destiny asked. She was turned all the way toward the window, away from me, her seat belt strained across her shoulder.

"It's white," I said, which was true. There was no way I wanted to get into telling her Pidge was in *my* mom's car . . . no way I wanted to get into telling it, or thinking about it either.

"I hate to say this, Jason, but if he did have an accident it would have been cleared by now. There'd be nothing to see."

"I know." Immediately I had a vision of the white car totaled, the silent figure on the stretcher. Please don't let that have happened to Pidge. Please. We'd passed the broken divider a while back but neither one of us had mentioned it.

"Is it all right if I talk," Destiny asked, "or would you rather be quiet?"

"Quiet is bad," I said. "It leaves too much room for thoughts." I couldn't remember ever feeling as nervous as I did at that moment.

"I was just thinking," Destiny said. "You and Meeker and Pidge are real buddies. But you're all so different."

"I know. I guess I'm the one in the middle. Pidge is my friend, and Meeker's my friend, so it works out." I glanced at her and smiled a little, knowing there was more to it than that, but not exactly sure what.

"I like the way you both look out for Pidge," she said. "It's nice for him."

"It's nice for us, too."

We were at the end of the Pasadena Freeway now and there was Meeker's Corvette parked just around the corner from Blair High. I pulled up beside him and he stuck his hand out of the window and pointed along Glenarm in the direction of our street.

"I'm headed this way," he said.

"I won't be long," I called.

"Don't be," he said. "Good night, Destiny."

"Good night."

I drove past him, heading north.

Except for the usual bustle of Old Town the city streets were quiet. On Ridgemore Road the softball players had gone home and the step-sitters had moved inside. There was a light on on Destiny's porch and another slitting out from behind the miniblinds in a front room.

I jumped out of the car to open the door for her but she opened it herself, so I leaned into the back seat and took out the box with the crystal rose.

"What's this?" she asked and I saw the surprise on her face.

I put the gift in her hands the way I'd imagined doing and I said, "It's for you. Happy birthday."

"Oh, Jason. As if you haven't done enough." We were still standing on the path. Through the open windows of the house next door I heard voices. Across the street a man walked his dog. He stopped while it sniffed the lamppost and then used what I supposed was somebody else's front grass. I stood thinking, Damn, there's Pidge to worry about, and people talking next door, and a man with his dog, and I still haven't kissed her. It must be destiny. And then I thought, Don't *you* start making jokes out of her name. Not that this was any joke.

"I'll open this upstairs in my room," Destiny said. "Thank you, Jason. I hope everything's OK about Pidge."

She was going. I touched the red ribbon, dark as blood under the streetlights. "This . . . what I bought you . . . I showed it to Pidgy. He liked it a lot."

I knew I was talking to keep her with me a few more minutes though Meeker had warned me to hurry.

"I know I'll like it a lot, too." She leaned over and for just a second I felt the warm smoothness of her lips on mine. I touched the sweet, thick braid of her hair. Then she was gone, running lightly up the steps, that thick, sweet braid jouncing against her neck. She waved from the front door and I waved back, and then stood quiet for a few seconds, still tasting her kiss, every bit of me melting at the thought of her. I didn't want to leave. But I had to.

· · ·

Meeker was coming across the street as I drove along Oakdale and I pulled up beside him.

He nodded back toward his own house. "I put the Corvette in our carport," he said. "And I told Babs and Harry I was home and I was going up to my room. I did go up. Of course I came down again. Not that they heard me anyway. They were deep in a bridge game with the Warwicks."

"What is all this cloak-and-dagger stuff?" I asked. "Why didn't you just say you were going out to look for Pidge?"

"I could have. They wouldn't have heard that either. I guess it just isn't my habit to give information away for free."

That I knew.

"Have you checked if the car's there?" I asked.

"I haven't looked yet. Anyway, we couldn't tell till you open the garage."

I drove into our driveway, Meeker pacing beside me. The smell of Mom's jasmine hung heavy in the night. In the shrubbery the crickets were chirping their heads off.

"Hey, the garage doors are already open," Meek

said. "And there's your mom's car." I saw the car at the same time and stepped on my brakes. "He didn't take it after all," Meek went on. "Messed up the whole night for all of us. I swear, when I see that guy . . ."

I jumped out of Dad's car and began running up the rest of the driveway.

Meek and I were almost at the garage now. I could read Mom's rear license plate. I could see the remains of an old bumper sticker about saving African elephants.

"What — ?"

I stopped. Stopped talking and stopped moving.

"Someone's in the car," I whispered. "It's Pidge. What does he think he's doing sitting there in the dark? Sitting in the driver's seat?"

Meek and I were hurrying now. "Pidge!" I called. "Pidge!" And that terrible nervousness came back, worse, a hundred times worse, than before.

CHAPTER 5

It was dark in the garage. I ran forward, between my mom's car and the wall, and switched on the bright overhead light.

Pidge was slumped in the driver's seat, wearing his red St. Jo's windbreaker. He turned his head toward me. There was a cut about an inch long above his right eye.

"Pidgy," I whispered. "What have you done to yourself?"

And then I saw the front of my mother's car.

"Oh, no!" I groaned.

I opened Pidge's door. "Are you all right? Jeez! What happened?"

I took another couple of shaky steps to really look at the damage to the car.

Behind me Meeker was saying, "What's going on? Why are you sitting in the car, Pidge? Are your legs broken or what?"

"No, my legs are all right," Pidge said.

Well, mine sure weren't.

I could hardly believe what I was seeing. The right fender on Mom's car was smashed all the way to the door. The right headlight had a triangular hole in it big enough to stick your fist through, if you were stupid enough to stick your fist through it. I leaned back against the wall and put my hands over my eyes. "I'm sick," I muttered. "I think I'm going to throw up. How could you go and trash my mom's car like this? What am I going to tell her?"

Pidge was standing beside me now, running his hands across his blond stubble of hair. I touched the cut and he screwed up his face.

"We better get you to an emergency room," I muttered. "This could need a couple of stitches."

He brushed my hand away. "Naw. I'll stick a Band-Aid over it."

Meeker was walking around the car now, his hands in his pockets. He stopped at the front and gave a disbelieving whistle. "What did you hit? A brick wall?"

"No." Pidge's lump of an adam's apple moved up and down as he swallowed. "Another car."

"Jeez!" I was standing straight now, all right.

"A parked one," Pidge said quickly. "I was making the turn down there on Lopez. You know, Jase? It's narrow . . ." He spread his hands about four inches apart. "There aren't any streetlights, either, and no parking on one side. But when I came around there was this little car . . . it was black . . . I didn't see it. One of those little black Mercedes . . ."

Meeker held up his hand. "Wait! Wait! You hit a black Mercedes? Are you saying what we think you're saying?"

I let myself slide down the garage wall. No kidding, I hadn't the strength to stay upright.

"It was one of those little ones," Pidge said again. "It shouldn't have been there."

"Just a little seventy-thousand-dollar 560 SL," Meeker said. "Ye gods! What did the owner say? Was he hurt? I'm surprised you're here. I'd have thought he would have killed you on the spot."

"There was nobody in the car. I guess the owner was in the house. It made a lot of noise . . . a sort of grinding."

I shuddered.

"But those houses are so far back," Pidge went on. "Maybe somebody came out. But I was gone by then. I just took off. It was your mom's car, Jase, and I didn't want you to get into trouble. I thought the best thing was to bring it back here."

I knew Pidge wasn't making excuses. That would be exactly the way he'd figure it. He'd protect me.

"I don't think I did it that much damage," he said.

"I'll just bet," Meeker said. "Did you even call Valerie?"

"Uh-uh. All I did was come here and sit."

I was talking to myself. "My mom loves this car. She's had it forever and ever."

Pidge had edged himself closer to Meeker. "Do you think I'll lose my license, Meek? I was thinking I might."

"You'll lose it all right if you get caught, that's for sure."

"But if I can't drive, what'll I do? Jase?"

"How do I know?" I said. "You should have called the police."

"Maybe he should and maybe he shouldn't," Meeker said. "We all need time to think about this."

"Please," I said sarcastically.

They were both silent as I went around the car again. I straightened the buckled license plate with my toe.

"Who's going to break the news to my mom?" I asked. "You, Meek? You were so sure I should let Pidge take it. Are you going to tell her, Pidge? I wasn't supposed to worry, oh, no."

"Let's go in the house," Meeker said. "Pidge needs to sit down. He doesn't look so good."

I glanced over at him, all pasty-faced. The cut was still oozing a little blood and one eye was closed like Long John Silver's.

"We'd better have somebody look at that," I said. "Come on, let's go."

Meeker shook his head. "They'll ask a lot of questions about how he got it and stuff. We'll clean it off ourselves." He grabbed Pidge's arm. "You've had worse on the football field, huh? Remember when the Cleary guy's cleat almost took your ear off?"

They were headed out of the garage. I pushed past them and unlocked our front door.

The living room lamp had come on with its automatic timer. I switched on more lights and Pidge sat down on the edge of the couch the way he always does, toes turned in.

I examined the cut. "Go get a Band-Aid and the Bactine," I told Meeker.

He brought a cotton pad, too, and we swabbed off the blood and pulled the edges of the cut together.

"Where was your seat belt in all this?" I asked.

"On," Pidge said. "I just bumped the steering wheel, that's all. It's OK. It hardly hurts anymore. It's just, you know, I'm worrying about what's going to happen next. About the car and my license and all."

I flopped into Dad's big leather chair, still holding the Bactine and the blood-soaked swab. "I don't know. We have to do something."

"Is there any of that ginger ale left?" Meeker asked.

"Maybe. I don't know." Typical Meeker. At a time like this, he thinks of ginger ale.

Pidge and I sat, not looking at each other, till Meek came back with three cans of drinks. He sat opposite me in Mom's chair, cradling a can in his hands, looking pleased with himself.

"I came up with something," he said. "Remember Floyd Taglia? He's a good friend of mine. You got to remember him. He used to play third base for McDonald's, back in Pony League when you were still playing Little League, Jase."

"Naw."

"I don't remember him either," Pidge mumbled. "Are you sure it was McDonald's? There was a guy named Floyd played for Michelin. . . ."

I gave him a despairing look. Sometimes Pidge could just about drive you crazy.

"Floyd Taglia's a killer mechanic and body man," Meeker said. "He lives up in the canyon. He's married and he's got a little cabin up there and he works on cars and trucks and stuff. He's hot. I swear, Jase, he could fix your mom's car up so good she'd never know anything happened."

"She'll know, all right, because I'm going to tell her. First thing tomorrow morning, if I can even hold out that long."

"I can understand that you want to, Jase. But think about it. Wouldn't it be better to tell her what happened *after* her car is fixed? That way, the car'll be looking just like new and she won't get so freaked."

"No kidding, Meek? Is this guy that good?" Pidge asked.

"He's a genius." Meeker jumped up. "I could give him a call. No harm in that. I could tell him the damage and see what he has to say. OK, Jase?"

"Yeah," Pidge said. "If he can fix it up and we don't have to tell, I wouldn't lose my license, huh? Let Meek call, Jase, OK? Please."

All of a sudden I was so exhausted I could hardly hold my head up. It was supposed to have been such a great night. And all I'd done was lend my friend my mother's car. That wasn't so terrible, was it? How had everything gone so wrong?

Meeker was leafing through the phone book. "Taglia? Taglia?" he muttered. "Here it is. Jason, this guy can work miracles. I've seen. I drove up there one day with Chris McNally . . ." And all the time he was talking he was dialing, then listening.

"Do you know it's ten minutes past twelve midnight?" I asked. "This Floyd . . ."

Meeker lifted his hand for quiet. "Hello? Is this Floyd Taglia? Yeah, yeah, I know it's late." He held the phone away from his ear and crossed his eyes at us, then said, "No. This *is* an emergency." He tossed the phone from hand to hand, grinning, while the voice yammered away on the other end. There must have been a pause.

"It's Gavin Meeker," Meek said quickly. "I was out at your house with Chris McNally, remember? You fixed up his Camaro when he pulverized it. That's right." He winked at Pidge and me. "Well, it's not my problem. It's my friend's. His mom's car got banged up a bit." Pause. "Sure we got money." Pause. "There's a busted front fender and a smashed headlight. No biggie."

He listened. "We'd rather bring it tonight. We don't want a lot of people seeing us, if you know what I mean. OK?" He nodded, grinned at us, said, "See you in a half hour," into the phone, and hung up.

He punched the air with a triumphant fist. "He's on."

"It's going to work out, Jase," Pidge told me. "Meeker's getting it fixed."

"OK now, how much money have we got between us?" Meeker demanded, and answered first. "I myself have forty-six bucks."

Pidge frowned. "I thought you had a whole lot more than that."

"I got more. In the bank, though, not with me. How much have you got, Jase?"

"Here." I tossed him my wallet. "Whatever's left. I took it all with me tonight." Tonight seemed so far away I could hardly remember it.

Meeker counted out loud. "Ten, twenty, twenty-four bucks. That's it?"

"That's it."

"Great," Meeker said sarcastically. "So far we have seventy dollars. Pidge?"

"I've got eighteen dollars and I still owe you ten for the two tickets for the club."

"Forget that," Meeker said. "It's all going in the same pot. Eighty-eight dollars. I wonder will he do it for that? Face it, his rates have to be lower than your average service station."

"Or maybe extra for keeping his mouth shut," I suggested.

Pidge heaved himself up. "Whatever it costs, I'll pay you guys back. I have the parking job with Jason, and next week I'm working days at the Hot Dog Diner. If I still have my license, that is.

But they're not going to take it away now, huh, Jase?"

"I guess not," I said. "You know, the best thing would just be if I told my parents. I could say I was driving and . . ."

"Hit-and-run, Jase. You want to lose *your* license?" Meeker asked, whistling soundlessly and staring at the ceiling.

"We trust you, Jason," Mom had whispered when they were leaving. "Some of the people in the office tell me I'm crazy to leave a sixteen-year-old kid alone in the house while we're gone, and I tell them, 'You don't know this sixteen-year-old kid.'" She'd tweaked my hair. And now her sixteen-year-old kid had really messed up.

"If we do it this way," Meeker said, "Floyd fixes the car, we pay him what we've got and give him an IOU for the rest. We put the car back and nobody's in trouble."

"Sure. And what about the poor guy with the Mercedes?"

"He'll call his insurance agent." Meeker grinned. "And he'll never, never leave his car on a no-parking street again."

"I dunno, Meek." I bit my lip. One time my grandma knit me a sweater. There was a loose piece of yarn on the cuff and I pulled it and the cuff began unraveling. I pulled a little more and the whole sleeve started coming away, row after row. It was the oddest feeling. I was getting that same odd feeling now.

"Aw c'mon, Jase, be a pal!" Pidge said. "I don't want *my* mom to know about this either. She's got enough problems."

I believed it. With a dead husband, four kids, and a go-nowhere job, Pidge's mom never had anything *but* problems.

I plucked at my sleeve, looking for a loose thread that wasn't there. "OK," I said. "Let's go."

We decided that I'd drive Mom's smashed-up Ford and Meeker would follow with Pidge in Dad's Buick. I reversed carefully down the driveway.

Meeker peered at me through the open window of Dad's car. "All set?" Meek asked. "Wagons — roll!" I realized I'd never seen him look happier. Suddenly and certainly I knew: Meek was enjoying this. This was his kind of excitement. We were breaking the law, and for once Meeker was not bored.

CHAPTER 6

I was worried that the broken headlight wouldn't work, but it did. I was worried that Mom's car wouldn't make it up the hill toward the San Gabriels and the beginning of the canyons. But it did, and that made me feel a little better. Whatever damage was done seemed to be on the outside. Maybe Floyd, the super mechanic, could fix it after all.

It was dark up here with the mountains looming black against the sky, the city below, the headlights of Dad's car dimly following. Only the stars were bright, brighter than I'd ever seen them, except when we were camping.

I stopped at the top of Altadena Drive to let Meeker pass, since he knew where we were going.

He waved as he went. I swear he looked as if we were off on a midnight picnic.

The knowledge of how much he was enjoying this jolted me again. But it shouldn't have. I'd known Meeker long enough. And I knew his dad.

I don't remember how old I was when I first discovered that his dad, who'd enjoyed so many adventures, was a liar. Maybe Meeker discovered it at the same time. Before that, when we were little, I was so envious of Meek having Harry for a father. Harry would play football with us in his front yard and show us how he ran the winning touchdown in the Rosebowl in '68. I thought he was wonderful. He told us how he'd led his men up Hamburger Hill and how he spoke Russian so fluently he'd once been sent on a secret mission for the CIA.

I'd repeated all his stories to my parents. They must have known they were lies but they didn't say anything. I'm sure it was hard for my dad. I'm sure he knew I wished he was more like Harry. It must have been hard for Meeker, too, once he caught on.

He had stopped now in front of metal gates. I waited while he jumped out and opened them, then I drove through behind him. The driveway was rutted and little rocks jumped up to clatter against Mom's car. Great, I thought. There goes the rest of the paint work.

A dog was barking his brains out. I saw him in the headlights. He was a Doberman with lots of spit dangling from his teeth. I didn't like the crazy way he was throwing himself against his chain.

There was a small wooden house at the back of the littered yard. The door opened and a guy came out and picked his way through the jumble of car parts and old, dead tires.

"Shut up, Arnold!" he yelled and the noise subsided to a growl. I guessed the guy was Floyd. He must have pressed a switch by the side of the house because a floodlight came on, full beam.

Meeker and I got out. From the backseat of Dad's car I could hear Pidge's snores, loud and bubbly.

Floyd came toward us. He was bare-chested and so skinny his jeans were in danger of falling at every step. I've never seen hair as blond as his, so bleached out it was almost white.

"Which one of you guys is Mecker?" he asked.

"I am," Meek said.

So much for the two of them being friends. Saying he was somebody's friend when he wasn't was one of Harry's tricks. I didn't want to have that thought, but it came anyway.

"This the car?" Floyd padded toward it, his face expressionless.

"Yeah. My friend hit . . ." I began.

Floyd looked back at me and said sharply, "I don't want to know about it."

"OK," I muttered.

I watched him run his hand across the dented fender, feel along the side as gently as Dr. Bolton had felt along my leg the time we thought I'd broken it in the Trinity game.

"Mm." He got down and peered underneath, exploring whatever there was to explore before he stood up.

"Good car," he said.

I had the crazy thought that my mom would have been pleased that he approved.

His left hand disappeared over his right shoulder as he scratched his back. "I can get a headlight that doesn't look too new in the wrecker's yard. Bumper, too. This here'll have to be eased out." He patted the car's side, then went back to his scratching. "Tomorrow's Saturday . . ."

"Today," I corrected. He nodded.

"I could have it for you by Monday. Got a big job starting then, but this ain't much. Unless you want to wait a week?"

"We can't wait," I said.

He nodded. "That's what I figured. It'll cost you nine hundred and fifty bucks."

I gasped. "Nine hundred and fifty *dollars*?"

"No, pesos," Floyd said sarcastically.

Meeker was nodding. "Sounds reasonable. We'll pay you eighty-eight dollars now and give you fifty a week for . . ." He was counting on his fingers.

"*Adiós*." Floyd turned away.

Arnold started barking and leaping again and Floyd growled, "Shut up, mutt."

"Wait a second," Meeker said. "Look, you know me. I'm a friend of McNally's and he . . ."

"I don't care if you're a friend of Holy Moses. I work for cash on the line. No checks, no American Express, no catch-you-later."

"How about the eighty-eight dollars now so you can get started tomorrow — today — and the rest when we come for the car?"

Before Floyd could answer I said, "Hold on, Meeker. How do we know this guy can do a good job?" I pointed to the yard and the piles of junk. "I don't have a great feeling about this. For nine hundred and fifty bucks we could take the car to a regular body shop where they guarantee their work."

Floyd scratched the back of his neck and grinned. "You think so, huh? Try a couple of thousand, more like. And plenty of questions. They're always suspicious of kids." He stared hard at me, then crooked a finger. "Come on."

I went.

He was walking around the side of the house,

pushing through waist-high grass and weeds, with me behind and Meeker hard on my heels.

"Probably poison oak," Meeker whispered. "Did you see him scratch?"

"Mosquitoes," I said, swatting at the five or six that were buzzing round my head.

There was another yard in back, floodlit too, screened from the street by high hedges. A real cherry of a Datsun 300ZX sat under the light, paint gleaming.

"So?" I asked. "Nice car."

Floyd grinned. "You should have seen it four days ago. He's picking it up in the morning."

I nodded, getting the picture.

"This was a major job, though." Floyd picked a dead leaf off the glistening paint. "Yours is peanuts."

"So is it a deal, then?" Meeker asked him. "You start and you get the balance when we pick up the car?"

Floyd eyed us. "No way. I start when I get it all. You can leave it if you leave the eighty-eight bucks. It can sit till you come back."

"That's fair," Meeker said. "Give him the money, Jase."

"Just hold on." I grabbed Meeker's arm and pulled him to the side.

"Little conference, huh?" Floyd grinned. His teeth were smaller than the Doberman's but just as sharp. He walked back to the Datsun and stood admiring it, scratching his shoulder this time.

"I'm not leaving my mom's car on the chance that we'll come up with the rest of the money," I said. "Where are we going to get it?"

"Relax, will you?" Meeker said. "Like I told Pidge, I got money in the bank. I've got more than a thousand bucks. No problem."

"You do?" I was so relieved I could have hugged him which would definitely have been the wrong thing to do. "Thanks, Meek," I said. "I mean it. I'll pay you back every cent."

"I know. Don't worry about it."

I cuffed his shoulder. "Thanks," I said again.

The minute we stopped talking Floyd turned around. "Decisions, decisions," he said.

We pushed back through the weed jungle to the front yard and I gave him the eighty-eight dollars. He counted it twice.

"Don't we get a receipt?" I asked.

Floyd seemed to think that was pretty funny. "You think I might run off with your car and your money? If I was going to run with anything I'd take the 300ZX, believe me."

"We'll bring the rest of the cash in the morning," Meeker told him.

Floyd nodded. "And like I said, that's when I'll start."

"Just make sure you do a good job," I said, trying to sound tough.

Floyd showed his little Doberman teeth in another grin. "Close the gates after you. I'll be letting the mutt off as soon as you go."

I took one last look at Mom's poor smashed-up car and I wanted to run back and rescue it. But that's what we were doing, wasn't it? Rescuing it by getting Floyd to fix it. And he definitely was good. I made myself think about that Datsun 300ZX. Man, that thing looked so clean it could have been in a showroom window.

Pidge was still snoring gently in the back seat as I drove out of the yard. You didn't have to worry about a person with a cut on his head sleeping afterward, did you? No, that was only for a major bump. Besides, I thought, Pidge sleeps every chance he gets.

Meeker had waited to close the gates behind us. The very second he climbed into the car I heard the fury of Arnold, free at last and flinging himself against the fence.

"*Adiós*," I muttered.

Pidge would be happy, all right, when he woke up and we told him we'd left the car to be fixed. He'd be off the hook; he wouldn't lose his license. Face it, I'd be happy too. I'd be off the hook myself, and as for Mom, her car would be better than ever.

I might even have to dirty it up a bit so it didn't look so brand new.

"What time does your bank open?" I asked Meeker. I was feeling a bit lightheaded. "We might just as well stay up."

"It doesn't open till Monday," Meeker said.

"What?" I thought I'd heard wrong. "But all banks open Saturdays now. Oh, I get it, you can write a check and get someone to cash it tomorrow and . . ."

"It's a savings bank. I can't write checks. I have to go in and fill out a withdrawal."

I was driving so slowly we were almost stopped. Meeker had tipped his seat back and lay with his eyes closed.

"What are you talking about? You said we'd have the money first thing . . . You mean we won't?"

I pulled over by the curb and slammed the brakes on so hard that Pidge was bumped half off the backseat. His snores stopped. He sat up and gave a loud yawn. "Is this where the guy lives?"

"No," I said. "We've been, and left the car, and we need nine hundred bucks that we don't have."

"Will you just shut off the motor and shut up yourself and let me think," Meeker said.

"I'm sick of your thinking. It's your thinking and my listening that got us into this. I'm going back for Mom's car and . . ."

"And what?" Meeker asked. "It ought to be easier to get nine hundred bucks than two thousand."

"Nine hundred? Wow." Pidge whistled.

I leaned my head against the steering wheel. Maybe I could sell my camera. It should be worth at least seventy-five bucks. I could take it to one of those pawnshops. And I could call Grandma. She'd lend me some. She wouldn't even ask why I needed it. But she'd worry. She'd think I was in trouble. Well, I was. Mr. Nichols had asked me to paint his garage over the summer. I wondered if he would give me cash in advance. Why would he?

I stared ahead at the wide boulevards, lined with light, that ran down toward the city. They looked like airplane runways. No planes taking off, though. I wished we could take off and zoom away to a place where none of this had ever happened.

"I shouldn't have spent so much on that damn dinner tonight," I said. "It cost me a bundle." But suddenly I was remembering Destiny, and the guy at the piano singing and smiling up at us. I was remembering the kiss, and an ache tore inside me.

Pidge's breath was warm on the side of my face as he leaned close. "My little sisters have some cash in their piggy banks. I'm talking maybe thirty-five bucks between them. They'd give it to me. I couldn't ask my mom, though. Things are too tough at home."

He stretched across Meeker who was still flat out on the passenger seat. "I bet Harry would lend us whatever we need."

"Yeah! Harry!" I couldn't believe I hadn't thought of that.

Meeker scowled. "Naw. I don't want to tell him about this. He wouldn't want me pulling my money out of the bank."

"Oh?" Harry would know I'd pay Meeker back. He'd love to be in on this. He'd get a kick out of it. It wasn't because of the money that Meeker didn't want to ask him. This was Meeker's show. He didn't want Harry brought in.

"I guess I'll try calling my grandma," I muttered.

"You don't have to," Meeker said softly. "I know where we can borrow the money till I get to mine on Monday."

"You do?" I glanced at him in astonishment. He was smiling.

CHAPTER 7

"So where are we going to get the money?" I asked Meeker.

"From a friend of mine."

I kept my voice carefully calm. "Oh, another friend. What is this one? A moneylender? Will he break our legs if we don't pay on time? What does he charge for interest on nine hundred dollars, a thousand or two?"

Meeker pulled the floor lever and jolted himself upright. "You need to work on your sarcasm, Jase. You're not real good with it." But he was smiling and he reached out to punch my arm. "This guy's no moneylender. He's just a super-good buddy."

"What's his name?"

"Bobby Chu. You don't know him. He works out

with me at the gym. I'll call him as soon as we get back to the house."

I peered at the clock on the dash. "It's ten minutes to two now and you're going to call him when we get back to the house? He'll love that."

"No. It's OK. He works nights. I'll call him on the job. I do it all the time. It's real boring for him and he likes to get phone calls. And in case you've forgotten, Jase, we're in a hurry for the money."

"I haven't forgotten anything," I said. Not Mom's car sitting up there in the trashy yard, not Floyd's hard, sharp voice telling us he wouldn't start till he got all of the money.

I let off the brake and put the car in drive.

"Where does your friend work, Meeker?" Pidge asked. "They must pay him a lot if he has all this money. I've been looking for that kind of job myself."

"You wouldn't like it. It's in one of those all-night minimarkets and they pay him minimum. I'm not even sure where it is."

"So how come he can lend us this much?" I asked. "Is he pushing crack on the side?"

"Uh-uh." Meeker shook his head. "Clean as a whistle. But he's a thrifty little nerd and a major workaholic."

"It's real nice of him to lend us the money," Pidge said.

"Well, he's a friend. You'd lend me money if I needed it, wouldn't you, Pidge?"

"Sure. If I had it," Pidge said.

Meeker grinned back at him. "That'll be the day, Pidgy." He glanced at me. "Besides, I'll tell Bobby it's only for two days. He won't lose even ten cents interest."

"We should pay him some anyway," I said. I was wondering why I'd never heard Meek mention this Bobby Chu if they were this tight. Still, I knew Meeker did spend a lot of time at the gym. He'd gone bowling with a bunch of the guys from there a couple of times.

"Remember when Harry raised two million bucks to train our mercenaries to overthrow that South American dictator?" Meeker asked me, his voice mocking. I glanced at him quickly, but didn't speak.

Pidge nodded. "I remember. That Harry's something."

"Two mill's major bucks," Meeker said. "We're only shooting for a measly nine hundred. That's peanuts for a son of Harry's."

Yeah, I thought. But Harry's two mill was probably one of his lies. This nine hundred's for real.

We were passing Destiny's street. I peered along it, seeing the dark bulk of her house, imagining her asleep, thick hair spread across her pillow. Was she dreaming? Smiling? Had she liked the crystal rose? Had she liked me?

We passed a police car, hiding with its lights out. I saw the shadow of two cops in it and I thought their heads turned to check us out. Automatically I glanced at the speedometer, but it was fine. We even had our seat belts on. Still, I was glad when the black and white didn't come after us. Not that we were doing anything wrong, but they might think we were.

I made the turn onto our street.

"I'll go get Bobby's phone number," Meeker said. "You guys stay put."

"I need to go to the bathroom," Pidge said.

"We'll be in the house, Meek," I said. "You'll have to come in to use the phone anyway."

Pidge suddenly leaned forward and hung one heavy arm over Meeker's shoulder and the other over mine. "You guys, I'm sorry I'm giving you all this trouble. If only I hadn't . . ."

"It's OK, Pidgy," Meeker said. "We're having a . . ." He stopped. "We're handling it." I swear he'd been going to say "We're having a blast," and changed it at the last second.

We watched him lope across the street and then I pulled Dad's car into the driveway and Pidge and I went in the house.

Everything was dark. The living room lamp had

clicked itself off at midnight so I found the hall switch.

Pidge went straight off to examine himself in the gilt-framed mirror.

"Criminy!" He spat on his finger and rubbed at the streaks of dried blood on his face. "This thing has bled some more. I look like the night of the living dead."

"You use the downstairs bathroom," I said. "I'll go upstairs."

In Mom and Dad's room I looked at myself in the full-length mirror doors. There wasn't a bleach or a detergent on the market that could save these white pants. Floyd's grass had done them in. I'd even picked up a grease mark somewhere that zigzagged like a lightning bolt down the left leg. Behind me, Mom and Dad's king-size bed was reflected, smooth and empty. The red figures on their little clock changed: 2:05. I thought of them in their hotel room in San Francisco, innocent, unworried, still thinking they could trust their kid to take care of things at home. And look what I'd done.

I clicked off the light before I could think about it anymore.

I was still in the bathroom when the doorbell chimed. Meeker was back.

When I ran down the stairs I saw that Pidge had let him in and that Meek had changed into jeans and a dark blue hooded sweatshirt with front pockets. Pidge's face was all shiny and smooth, the way it always got after he washed it. It hadn't changed that much since we sat next to each other in kindergarten. "Gerber Baby," Meeker called him.

Meek reached up and touched the Band-Aid above Pidge's eye. "Does it still hurt?"

"Ow!" Pidge slapped his hand away. "Of course it still hurts. What did you think?"

"Did you get the phone number, Meek?" I asked.

"Got it and called him already. Harry and Babs are sleeping like a couple of mice. Bobby said sure, come on down." Meeker pulled a slip of paper from the pocket of his sweatshirt. "It's the Sunshine Market in Alhambra. I've got directions. Let's go."

"You mean we're going right now? The guy has nine hundred bucks in his wallet and . . ."

"He's going to give us a check that we can take in to Wells Fargo in the morning. It opens at nine."

"Can't he just give it to you tomorrow at the gym?"

"Jason! What's the matter with you? Tomorrow at the gym is four o'clock or later. We get the cash first thing and run it up to Floyd and he gets started. Right?" He held up the paper. "Alhambra. Sixty-four thirty-four Poplar."

I nodded. "Did you tell him we'd give him an IOU?"

"No." Meeker rolled his eyes. "He doesn't want an IOU. He didn't ask for an IOU."

I felt like arguing. "He should have one. I'd want . . ."

"Oh, shoot . . . give me a pen."

I reached him one from beside the phone. He turned over the address paper, printed IOU $900, and signed *Gavin Meeker.*

"OK?"

"We should sign it, too," I said.

"What for? It's me you'll owe the money to, not Bobby. I trust you. Let's go."

The Warwicks' fat, furry cat was sleeping on the hood of Dad's car. She'd settled for the night and wasn't happy when I shoved her off.

"Take Atlantic," Meeker said. "Hang a left on Main."

It was weird driving past the shuttered shops and sleeping houses. I don't think I'd ever driven this late, or actually this early in the morning. Except for the time my family went to London and we had to leave the house at four A.M.

Alhambra is the next town southwest of Pasadena. It's almost like Chinatown now since so many Asian immigrants moved in. Pretty soon we began cruising past shops with Chinese signs above the doors, or maybe Vietnamese or Korean. I wouldn't know the difference.

"Turn left here," Meeker said, "at the dragon." The dragon was on the corner of a restaurant with a pagoda roof.

Pidge turned to stare out of the back window. "Wow, look at the teeth on that thing, will you?"

"Listen, Meek. Are you sure about this?" I asked. "Everything's closed."

"The Sunshine Market isn't. Didn't I just call Bobby? Head right at the stop sign. It should be Poplar."

It was. And right away I could see the market, small with a little parking lot, brightly lit. The sign was in English, but there were subtitles. The specials pasted on the windows were in a couple of languages, too. The parking lot was empty.

"No wonder your friend likes somebody to talk to nights," I said.

"Do you want us to come with you, Meek?" Pidge asked, leaning forward.

"Naw. Neither of you looks like somebody a guy ought to lend money to. Stay put."

He'd slammed the door and taken a couple of steps when I saw the IOU where he'd left it on the seat between us.

"Hey!" I leaned across, rolled down the passenger window, and fluttered it outside. "You forgot something."

Meek came back, took it, and slid it into his

pocket. "Keep the noise down, OK? It's three o'clock in the morning."

The radio *was* on fairly loud. I turned the knob till I found a talk show, put it on low, and rolled up the window. Some woman was talking on the air about how the Chinese government had shown itself in its true colors the way it handled the dissidents, and the host, who had one of those plummy English voices, was asking her what she would have done. "What action would you have taken, madame?"

I wondered if Bobby Chu was Chinese and if he was glad he was here and not there. I bet he wouldn't have had a checking account with megabucks in it in Beijing.

I tried to see through the market windows but there were too many pasted-on signs covering the glass. Behind me Pidge began to snore gently. I swear, the single biggest difference between Meek and Pidge is what happens when they get bored, I thought. Meek does something outrageous and risky. Pidge sleeps.

I was tired, too. I tried to stay alert and think things out, step by step the way Meeker does, but my mind kept slipping. This was such a strange place to have an all-night market, like an oasis in the desert, spotlighted in the surrounding darkness. If I had money saved the way this guy had, I for sure wouldn't be working here. **OK**. Think things through. In the morning we'd cash Bobby Chu's check and head for Floyd's. Floyd would get started. Probably he'd go right away and buy the light and the fender. We'd come home and crash for twenty-four hours or so. Maybe I'd call Destiny and she'd say, "Last night was really great, Jason. I loved . . ."

Meeker was coming out of the market, walking toward the car, his hands stuck in the pockets of his sweatshirt, his head down. I thought he'd be waving the check, strutting. . . .

"I don't think he got it," I said.

He jerked open the door and Pidge wakened.

"Go," Meeker told me.

"Did you get the check?" Pidge asked.

"Did he . . . ?" I began.

Meeker interrupted. "I've got the money. Let's boogie."

I grinned at him. "Great!" I said, and then I started the car and drove out of the parking lot.

"Left here," Meeker said in a quiet, calm voice. "Drive slowly. Take it easy. Don't speed." His voice was still low and reasonable. So why was I getting this bad feeling?

We drove for a couple of miles with only the radio talking. The radio, and Pidge asking, "Meek? Meek?" No answer. Something was very wrong. My heart began to race.

"Pull in behind that truck and shut the motor," Meeker said.

I did. We were on a silent residential street lined with parked cars. It couldn't be Pasadena because in Pasadena there's no overnight parking. Oak trees stretched their branches, meeting in an arch, their shadows streaking the pavement under the streetlights. Someone had T.P.'d one of the biggest trees a long time ago and the torn scraps of toilet paper still hung, forgotten, from the top branches.

On the radio the plummy voice was saying, "I take it you don't think . . ."

"Is everything OK, Meek?" Pidge whispered.

Everything was not OK. I knew it.

I grabbed his arm. "What happened, Meek? What happened?"

Meek didn't answer. He leaned across and switched off the radio and stared at me through the silence.

CHAPTER 8

"You didn't get the check," I said, relieved some-how, though I guess I shouldn't have been. No check meant no money meant no car. But hadn't Pidge just asked and hadn't Meeker said he got it? "Was the manager there? Did Bobby get in trouble for having a visitor?" I asked. "What?"

Meeker took his hands out of his pockets. I realized he'd had them jammed in there, out of sight, since he came out of the Sunshine Market. Except when he got in the car and had to open the door. Now he took a handful of money from the left-hand pocket and put it on the seat beside us.

"What . . . ?"

Pidge's head poked between us. "He gave you cash money? Nine hundred bucks of cash money?"

From his right-hand pocket Meeker took something else, something bundled up, maybe a dark-colored sweater, and stuffed it down between the seat and the door. Then he was pulling out more bills, singles, tens, twenties. More and more, heaping them, green and wrinkled, under the light from the streetlamp. A few slid off the top to drift down to the floor of the car.

Pidge poked at the pile, shifting the balance, knocking more to the floor. "Are they *real*?"

I gripped the wheel with both hands. "You robbed the market, Meeker." It wasn't a question. I knew.

Meeker turned to face me. "I did not. I borrowed the money. I'm going to give it back. On Monday."

"Sure," I said. "And Bobby Chu went along with it. Bobby Chu said, 'Go ahead, Meeker, take what you need.'" My grip on the wheel was so tight now that my arms tingled pins and needles all the way to my shoulders.

"Not exactly," Meeker said.

"I bet not exactly."

I was thinking things through now, all right, my mind sorting and discarding. "You never called him, did you? He never said he'd give you a check. You knew he'd be there by himself tonight because he's always there by himself. You planned to rob him all the time."

"No." Pidge's voice was so loud it jolted me.

"Sh!" I warned, peering nervously out of the window into the darkness beyond the street-lights.

"Meek wouldn't do a thing like that," Pidge said.

"Yes, he would. But what I can't figure is . . . how? Bobby Chu knows you, or was that a lie, too? He'd recognize you right away. He'd call the cops unless . . ."

I leaned across Meeker, my fingers searching for whatever he'd stuffed down the side of the seat. He didn't try to stop me as I tugged it free and shook it out. It was a knitted ski mask, black, with holes for the eyes and mouth.

"You wore this," I said.

Meeker nodded and half smiled. "It's Harry's. It's the one he bought in Sports Chalet the time he wanted to go to the IRA funeral, for those Irish Republican Army terrorists who were shot. Remember?"

"You stupid idiot, Meeker." I got my fingers in the eyeholes, stretching and jerking at the black wool. "What have you done? Robbery! Look at all this money." I swiped at the pile, fluttering it in all directions. "And you know what? I'm your driver. Pidge is . . . Pidge is your accomplice. You stupid . . ."

The mask wouldn't tear. I plucked blindly at its

edges, looking for a thread to pull the way there'd been on Grandma's sweater, so I could destroy it, make it disappear. Meeker watched me as I rolled down the window and pitched the mask into an oleander hedge.

I was panting as though I'd run a marathon.

"Feel better?" Meeker asked.

"I damned well don't," I said.

"Did you mean to throw that away, Jase?" Pidge asked anxiously. "Should I go get it?"

"No." I took a deep breath. "You wore the ski mask and what else did you have, Meeker? The guy didn't just hand over all this money because you said 'please.'"

"He gave him the IOU," Pidge said, but Meek didn't answer. For a second I saw the dark steel barrel, the polished handgrips of the gun in his hand. "Harry's," he said and tossed it carelessly into the backseat. "Catch, Pidge."

I was up on my knees, my hands reaching out toward the shining arc of the gun, but Pidge had it. Big awkward Pidge with the quick reflexes. Pidge who had such safe, mammoth-sized hands he could have been a receiver if he'd had more speed. But it wasn't a football he was holding now. He was examining the gun.

"Point it away from us, Pidge," I said quietly. "Give it over here to me."

"Relax, Jase," Meeker said. "The thing isn't loaded. But don't mess with it anyway, Pidge."

"I know enough not to mess with it. I know not to point it at anybody. Sometimes you guys act as if I'm stupid or something."

I was still up on my knees. My throat was dry, my heart pounding. Meeker had done crazy things before but nothing criminal, nothing like this. "Are you sure the gun's not loaded?" I asked.

"I told you," Meeker said. "Harry believes in safe firearm habits. Did you think I'd threaten Bobby Chu with a loaded gun? Give me a break."

"See, Jase?" Pidge broke it open and showed me the empty cylinders.

I let myself sink back into the seat. An oak leaf fell with a whisper onto the hood of Dad's car, and I remembered Floyd carefully picking the leaf off the Datsun 300ZX. I scratched at my forehead and felt the bump of a mosquito bite. That, this — it was all a nightmare.

"I don't understand, Meeker," I said, holding on to the steering wheel again. It was like a life raft and I was going through the rapids. If I let go of it, I'd drown. "You took Harry's gun and ski mask and you robbed that market. Have you any idea how serious this is? This isn't like taking a golf cart from the club and driving around in it for a while. Or . . . or taking Mrs. Costello's tomatoes. You could go to jail for this. We all could. This is armed robbery, man."

"We're not going to jail because we're not going to get caught. No way. And it's not robbery if we're just borrowing."

I bent forward, leaned my head on my arms, and closed my eyes. "What about the poor guy who owns the market?" I asked at last. "He's out nine hundred bucks."

"I don't think I got that much. And he's only out till Monday. Besides, he's a jerk. Bobby's been asking him to put one of those alarm buttons under the counter in case they got robbed. He wouldn't spend the bucks." Meeker grinned. "I bet he spends them now." He was gathering up the money, cramming it all into the glove compartment, pulling more from his pockets, stuffing it in, too. The glove compartment wouldn't close. He put his weight on it; still a corner of a bill stuck out. I saw a 10 on it.

"What about Bobby?" I asked. "What did you do to him?"

"Shot him, of course," Meeker said, and Pidge gasped.

"Don't be loony," Meeker snapped. "Of course I didn't shoot him. The gun was empty, for Pete's sake. I locked him in the back room. Somebody'll find him pretty quick. There's a phone in there, but I pulled out the wires."

"Jeez, Meek, you thought of everything." Pidge sounded awed, maybe even admiring.

"Monday he gets the money in the mail, anonymously. No, he won't get it till Tuesday, but that's OK."

"No. It's not OK," I said.

Meeker ignored me and talked to Pidge. "You know, come to think of it, ripping off Mrs. Costello's tomatoes may have been worse. We didn't pay *her.*"

"But we only took three tomatoes," Pidge said quickly. "It wasn't real stealing. We just wanted to see if we could get in and out, with her always on guard and everything. It was just to see if we could do it."

Meeker nodded. "That's why I did this, too. More or less. Of course, mostly it was to get you and Jase out of a hole."

I started the car. "It's not OK," I said again, under my breath.

"But you don't think you got the whole nine hundred?" Pidge asked.

"It didn't seem like it. We'll count it when we get home." Meeker paused. "What do you think you're doing, Jason?"

"Turning," I said.

"You don't have to turn. Keep going along here. It should bring us out on Main and then head straight up Atlantic and . . ."

"We're taking the money back," I said. "Now."

The street was narrow, like the one Pidge was driving on when he smashed Mom's Ford Fairlane and started all this. Cars were parked along it bumper to bumper; they didn't make turning easier. I backed out of the driveway I'd nosed into.

"No way," Meeker said.

"We put the cash back in the register or wherever you got it," I said. "If Bobby's still in the room we let him out. If we're lucky maybe we can level with him, and since you're his friend . . ."

"If, if, if. If he's mad and calls the cops we're done for," Meeker said.

I was concentrating on not hitting a parked van that said *Pan Plumbers — We'll Leave Your Drains as Clean as a Whistle* in white letters on the side. I'd just edged around it with a half inch to spare when Meeker leaned over, pushed the gear lever into park, and pulled the key out. Our car stalled. I fast put on the emergency.

"Look, Jason," Meeker said. "I'm not getting in a bunch of trouble over this. So far we're clean. And just remember, I did this for you . . . for you and Pidge."

We were right under a streetlight and I could see him clearly. I could see the thick, clean gleam of his hair, the little mole high on his cheek. I could see his eyes. Meeker has the nicest eyes. They're gray-blue, wide, honest. He always looks at you straight, too. No shifting away. Meeker has the kind of eyes you can trust. My mom was always saying that. Harry has that kind, too.

"You always wanted to pull something like this, Meek," I said. "Don't try to con me. I know you too well. You didn't do it for us, you did it for you."

The gray-blue eyes held mine. I stuck out my hand. "Give me the keys."

In the silence I heard police sirens scream not too far away. I heard them whine to a stop. There was a heavy whirr in the sky, red lights, a white beam pointing down, hovering, circling, not far away, maybe in front of the Sunshine Market.

"Sounds as if Bobby got himself out," Meeker said admiringly. "He's a smart little booger." He put the keys in my hand. "Here you go, buddy. But I don't think it would be too smart to go back there now."

CHAPTER 9

I fitted the key into the ignition.

"It would be a very smart move to stay right here," Meeker said. "Nothing's traveling in this street. We shouldn't either."

The car was filled with his tense excitement. I could smell it, sharp as ammonia. I'd smelled excitement on him before, when he and Pidge and I had been on one of his escapades, but never as strong as this.

"You . . . you're crazy." My words stumbled over one another.

"No, just playing possum," Meeker said, grinning widely. "Like this." He bent his head and covered his face with his hands, peering through his fingers.

I swallowed the hot rush of anger. "If you think

this is funny, Meek, you *are* crazy. Crazier than I thought."

Pidge tapped a fist filled with money against Meeker's shoulder. "Here. This pile flew in the back. There's fourteen dollars."

Meeker uncovered his face and sat up. He smoothed the bills and said seriously, "Thank you, Pidge."

"And you know what, Jase," Pidge whispered. "Meeker *did* do this for us. You and I are the only two in it. I think it was real nice of him. He's a real friend."

Meeker bowed in Pidge's direction. "Thank you. I'm glad somebody appreciates me."

"Shut up," I told him. "Just shut up."

Pidge was still mumbling behind us. "I should have been the one to go in the market, not Meek. I should have gone."

I swung around, ready to blast Pidge for saying something so dumb, but I didn't when I saw his face. His mouth was quivering the way it does when he's really upset. I could tell he was ready to bawl.

"You shouldn't have gone into the market, Pidgy," I said gently. "And Meeker shouldn't have either."

"You guys always have to take care of me," Pidge said.

Meeker stretched his arms and put his hands flat

on the roof, flexing his muscles. "True, true," he said cheerfully.

"It was all my fault in the first place, and now you and Jase are bailing me out again." Pidge covered his mouth with his knuckles.

"You betcha," Meeker said. "What else can we do for you?"

"Why don't you shove it, Meek," I said. "I'm sick of you acting like this is funny. You've got me in it, too, and Pidgy. You know how I try to look out for Pidgy. You know how he depends . . ."

Suddenly, before I knew what was happening, Pidge had wrenched open the door and was blundering through the oak leaves that littered the sidewalk.

"Pidge!" I called, but softly so as not to alarm the sleeping street.

"I'll get the money," he called back. "Me. Pidge. Nobody has to look out for me. I can look out for myself. You hear me?" I was afraid the whole street would hear him.

"Now look what you've done," Meeker said. "This is no night for Pidge to be running around loose."

"I'll go after him." Already I was out of the car, slowing to peer up at the sky where the helicopter turned in widening circles.

Meeker leaned out of the door. "Get back in here, Jason. Two guys running are easier to spot than one."

"I'll walk. You stay." I jerked my head toward the glove compartment. "Count your money. Think out your next move, why don't you?"

"Did anybody ever tell you you're an ungrateful jerk?" Meeker began to close the door, then pushed it open again. "Check the street name. All I need is for you to get lost. And don't be long, either." He disappeared as the door clicked closed, blending with the darkness inside.

I began walking fast in the direction Pidge had taken. He hadn't meant that about getting money. How could he, anyway? He just wanted to get away. Was he heading for home? But home was a heck of a distance. He wouldn't be crazy enough to try hitching, surely? Not when we'd just robbed a market. I walked faster. What way was that to put it, even inside my own head? We hadn't robbed anything. Meeker had. And he'd enjoyed every minute of it.

"This is no night for Pidge to be running around loose," Meeker had said. And this was no place either. The houses were seedy here and run-down. A dog roped to a tree in a front yard yapped at me as I passed. He looked like a rattle of bones. I moved from shadow to shadow, at the corner now, scanning the sidewalks in both directions. Which way had Pidge gone?

To the right the street led onto a main boulevard with an occasional rumble of traffic. The boulevard might even have been Atlantic; I'd lost all sense of direction. In Pasadena the mountains are always north, and if there's a smogless day and you can see them, you can get yourself on course. Here I could see nothing. To the left was a shadowy open area, with trees. It might be a park. I thought I saw the shapes of picnic tables. A guy who wanted to cry and not be seen could hide himself in there. But I didn't like the look of it. It was the kind of place you'd stay away from, even in daylight, even with a bunch of guys to back you up. I took a few reluctant steps in that direction.

It *was* a park, one of those small city ones that probably fifty years ago had been nice for family picnics and get-togethers. Now I could see the sagging wooden sign, giving the hours it was open. No dogs. No fires. No skateboarding. White graffiti were scrawled all over the sign and someone had gouged out **WARRIORS** in big, ragged letters. Below in black paint it said *We deal.* It was darker than dark in the park, beyond the reach of the streetlights.

"Pidge," I called, but so softly I could hardly hear myself.

A baseball bat lay on the thin grass. I picked it up and hefted it in my hand, but it was uselessly light, a kid's plastic toy, and cracked up the middle. I carried it anyway as I edged forward. There was nothing else. And then I heard voices, a man's, a woman's. There was a heavy scuffling sound and then a shot.

Sometimes, when a car backfires or when a cherry bomb bangs illegally on the Fourth, there's a second when your heart bangs with it and you think, "Somebody's shooting." But this couldn't have been anything but a gunshot. I knew. It was followed by another. My heart was banging now, all right.

Across the street, a light came on in the porch of the house nearest the park. I crouched behind a rusted barbecue on a stand. A man opened the front door of the house, probably opened it on a chain because the gap was no more than three or four inches. I saw the shine of his bald head, then the light went out and the door closed. Sweat trickled cold inside my shirt. I wanted to run over, to pound on the door, to shout to him to let me in, to keep me safe. But he wouldn't open up. He'd be too smart for that. And I couldn't ask him. There was some line I'd crossed tonight that could keep me locked outside with the rest of the bad guys forever.

Wait . . . someone was coming, running heavily between the dark shapes of the trees. The plastic bat was slippery with my sweat. I grabbed it with both hands, crouched lower, cursing my white pants, so easy to see, wishing I was home, safe, not here, crying maybe, I don't know. I peered around the rubble of the barbecue stand and saw the big, lumbering figure running, his head lowered, a tackle going in for the kill, a buffalo charging. He was clutching at his stomach.

"Pidge," I whispered and stood up.

Just as I said his name he dropped onto all fours, scrabbled to get to his feet again.

I ran toward him, chucking the baseball bat.

"Pidge. Pidgy!"

His head lifted. "Jase!" I thought I saw him try for a smile.

"What happened? Oh God, Pidge, what happened?" I got my hands under his armpits and helped him up. His weight made my legs buckle. I put an arm round his waist. The whole front of his shirt was soaked black, like oil. I tried to think that it couldn't be blood, because blood was red and this was black. But I knew it was. Blood.

"There was a guy — with a girl. I came . . ." The words stopped as pain twisted his face.

"Don't talk, Pidgy. The car's not far. Hold on to me."

I was taking his weight across my shoulders and the weight was pulling me down. We staggered past the park sign. No skateboarding. No fires. Why didn't it say no shooting? Now we were on the sidewalk. The same door of the same house opened but the porch light didn't go on, and when I called, "Please . . . my friend's hurt. . . . Can you . . . ?" the door closed fast. The scrawny dog yapped half-heartedly, wagged its scrawny tail.

Sometimes Pidge muttered words that I couldn't hear. Sometimes I heard. "Told him . . . give me money . . . need money . . . pointed gun . . ."

I almost let go of him. "You pointed the gun? You took the gun with you? Jeez, Pidge!"

"Guy put his . . . thought . . . wallet. Shot me."

The big head turned toward me. The cut above his eye was bleeding again through the Band-Aid but that blood was nothing, nothing. It was the blood on his shirt, on his hands, on me. "Not easy . . ." he said. "Not smart, like Meek."

I swallowed. "Meeker? Meeker's an idiot. Meeker . . . Don't think about it now, Pidge. Keep moving. Just don't give up on me."

I thought of all the houses we were passing, all the dark, empty windows. Who was watching us stumble through these yellow pools of lamplight? Who was dialing 911 . . . "Get the police. There was a shooting in the park." Would I hear the whish of the cop car wheels behind, the voices telling us to halt?

"That's good, Pidgy. Almost there. Almost there."

But maybe nobody was calling. Maybe in this neighborhood it was better to mind your own business. Maybe stuff like this happened all the time and the people who lived here said, "Let them kill each other off. What do we care. Good riddance." Maybe they said, "Lousy, rotten dopers."

Was Pidge heavier? He seemed heavier. My shoulders were numb where his weight lay across them. I had to order my own legs to keep moving, to not give up on me.

There was the car. But I couldn't . . . We were both sagging. Pretty soon I'd be crawling, dragging him behind, and then Meek was there, on Pidge's other side, taking the weight, easing the pain that knifed across and down my back. Meeker with his big, strong muscles that he worked on every night in the gym with Bobby Chu.

"He's shot," I gasped.

"Meek," Pidge whispered. "I tried to help. Tried to get . . ."

We were hauling him between us, his pigeon feet trailing. I looked back and saw the line of little drops, scarlet under the lamplight.

"Meek . . . I took Harry's gun. It's . . . in my pocket."

"OK," Meek said. "Everything's OK. Here's the car, Pidgy."

The back door was open. Meek must have opened it the minute he saw us coming. That was Meek, thinking ahead as usual.

I got in first and Meeker eased Pidge in to me. I laid his head on my knees and Meek bent up those big, heavy legs so he could cram them in, so the door would close.

"You guys?" Pidgy whispered. "You guys, I'm sorry."

CHAPTER 10

Meeker's driving, hauling us out of there. The car brakes are screeching, and he and I are yelling at each other although we're only a few feet apart and in the same car, yelling as if we've both gone suddenly deaf.

"There's a hospital in Alhambra," I'm shouting. "I don't know where it is or what it's called. Oh jeez! We'd better just stop at a gas station and call an ambulance."

"We'll make a run for Arcadia Methodist," Meeker yells back. He's breaking every speed record in the book. "We can go all the way along Huntington, it curves up."

I'm stroking Pidge's bristle of hair. Something's tangled in it but I just let my hand glide over it.

Sometimes he opens his eyes, looks at me as if he never saw me before, and groans. His hands keep feeling for his stomach, not finding it, groping up around his chest. Each time the car passes under a streetlight I can see the blood spreading, dripping.

I wrench off my shirt, though it's hard to do without disturbing Pidge, and I ball it up and put it on his stomach, pressing down a little, because I've seen them do that in movies and on TV. But when I do he screams and I let up on it fast.

Meeker's head jerks around at the scream and I get a glimpse of his face, white and frightened, pulled so tight he doesn't look like smart, cool Meeker at all.

"How far now?" I ask.

Sweat glistens on Pidgy's forehead and I wipe it off with the trailing sleeve of my shirt which is still sitting on his stomach, not doing any good.

"I dunno. I dunno. We're just coming up on Rosemead," Meeker says.

"If you see a cop car flag it, blast your horn," I tell him, but Meeker doesn't answer.

Where are all the cop cars anyway? The old joke never around when you need them. Maybe all the cops are at the Sunshine Market, talking to Bobby Chu. I don't know.

Pidge is breathing awful funny, loud as his snores, as if there's air stuck in his throat. I want him to cough. I cough for him. It doesn't help him any. I wiggle a hand underneath him and gently rub between his shoulders, though what good is that? It's just that it gives me something to do. I remember when our dog Mitzi was hit by a car, how I rubbed between her ears, sat there in the street with her head on my knees just like Pidgy's is now, rubbing her ears.

"Can't you drive any faster?" I yell to Meek.

"No."

Probably he can't. The car sounds like a 747 and we're swaying all over the boulevard. A good thing Huntington's wide — wide and empty, with stoplights Meeker is ignoring.

And all at once I realize it's awfully quiet in the car. What has happened to that raspy, air-mixed breathing? My heart goes wild, leaping and stopping. I bend over Pidge.

"Pidgy?"

I touch his forehead. It's clammy and cold. But it was clammy and cold before. That doesn't mean anything.

I put my face real close to his. I'm upside down to him. His mouth is open. I put my ear to it and I don't hear anything. Nothing.

"Meeker? Stop."

One of Pidge's arms is dangling over the seat, the hand on the floor. I raise it and hold it against my chest. It's so big it fills both my hands. I don't mean to check for a pulse, but I know how to do that and I'm doing it without meaning to. There is no pulse.

"Meek," I say again. "Stop."

CHAPTER 11

We are parked under a great, unfolding tree that screens the streetlights. Meeker is kneeling on the passenger seat. He and I stare at each other through the frightening shadows.

"You think he's *dead*?" Meeker's voice rises on the last word.

I nod and close my eyes.

"Maybe he just passed out from loss of blood," Meeker says. "People do that."

"Yeah. I bet that's it. He just passed out." I'm so relieved I could pass out myself. But what about that missing pulse? Well, I could have been holding his wrist in the wrong place. "So haul out of here again, Meek. I shouldn't have made you stop. We've got to get to the hospital."

"Does your dad have a flashlight?" Meeker asks and I say, "In the glove compartment."

Meeker's rooting around in there, money puffing out over his hands and wrists. "You're only wasting time, Meek," I yell. "Get going. We don't need a flashlight."

But Meek has found it and he turns it on and shades the beam with his hand. It wavers toward us, holding like a spotlight.

Pidgy's eyes are open, but they're not looking at anything. I see the Band-Aid we put on him earlier. I see the scar below his chin where he got cleated in the Queen of the Valley game and took four stitches. I see my shirt, still wadded up on his stomach, the darkness above and below it.

"He looks dead," Meeker says in a trembly voice. He turns off the light and I'm glad because Pidge is so scary, but I feel as if I can still see him even when the light's off, see the scar and the open eyes and everything. I think I'll always see him like that. Always.

Meeker and I are talking through each other, arguing, babbling.

"Mouth-to-mouth," I say. "I can do that. But it only works if you're flat. We'll have to lift him out."

"We can't lift him out. Are you nuts?" Meeker's shouting. "We don't want anybody to see him. Lay him flat on the seat."

"Why don't we want anybody to see him?" I mumble, but Meeker doesn't answer.

I get the door open and Meeker helps me ease myself out from under Pidgy's weight. I hold his head and lay it back gently on the seat.

My legs will hardly carry me around to the other rear door and I have to hold on to the car roof, to the taillights, to the fender. I get in again, kneeling in the space beside Pidge, lifting off my folded shirt and setting it on the floor, and I lean across him, hoping I'm not hurting him. Even the shirt hurt him. I try not to be heavy. His chest is as hard as a rock and wet against my skin.

Meeker's gotten back in front and he's bending over, telling me what to do. The words wash around me. I know what to do.

"Tip his head back. Get his chin up. Hold his nose," Meeker says. "Don't try chest CPR though."

I'm not going to. I know better than to touch down there where the bullet wound is.

I can't get him flat all the way because he's too long and his knees are bent and flopped over. But I have his top half straight.

"You drive, Meek," I shout. "Keep us moving."

I hear the car start as I get my mouth over Pidge's and start blowing. Twelve breaths per minute, one every five seconds. He smells of Brut aftershave. Oh, Pidgy, Pidgy.

Each time I empty the air from me into him I look to see if his chest is moving. It isn't. Come on, Pidge, come on.

Meek makes a sharp turn and Pidge slides half off. I get him back up. The weight in his pocket is Harry's gun, and I pull it out and drop it on the floor. Whatever street we're on now has brighter lights. I wish it didn't. I don't want to see this clearly. I don't want to see Pidgy's wide, staring eyes.

Blow, count, blow, count.

Coach Varien taught the team mouth-to-mouth. We used Resusci-Ann, a female dummy.

"Bet you wish you were doing this with Destiny instead of this old girl." That was Pidge, laughing at me, squinting through the sun, the grass of the football field dry and scratchy under my hands. The smells of summer.

"How long do I have to keep doing this, Coach?"

"Till the victim can breathe for herself."

"But she's a dummy, Coach. She ain't never going to breathe."

Pidge is never going to breathe.

I stop. I'm panting and exhausted.

"Do you think I'm doing this right?" I ask Meeker.

Pidge's head lolls to the side. I'm wet and slippery with his blood. "Maybe I didn't do it long enough. Maybe I'm not doing it right. Meek? Meek, you come and try. I'll drive."

His eyes meet mine in the rearview mirror. He shakes his head but he pulls in to the curb and stops. He leans over into the back. "Jason, it's no use," he says. "Pidgy's dead."

I nod slowly, because I know.

"Do you think . . . Should I close his eyes?" I ask, and Meeker says, "Do it."

I smooth the eyelids down the way I've seen it done a million times on TV. I fold Pidge's hands across his chest.

Meeker and I don't seem to know what to do next. We argue, halfheartedly. My legs are cramped and I want to get out of the back and stand up, but I'm afraid if I do Pidgy'll think I'm deserting him. He was always thinking that. I ease myself into a crouch.

"We should go on to Methodist Hospital anyway," I say.

Meeker shakes his head. "They can't do anything for him there."

"They can lift him out of the car, and put him in a bed and clean him up and get his mother," I say and I put my face down onto my bended knees and whisper, "Oh God, Meek. I'd forgotten about his mother!"

"I hadn't," Meek says. "Don't talk anymore. I have to think."

I'm too sick and too scared even to answer that.

"We should take him home," I say. My throat is closed and I can hardly get the words out. I slide up onto the seat next to Pidge, where his feet would be, except that they've slipped down onto the floor. I only have about three inches of space where I'm not touching him and I don't want to touch him because now he isn't Pidgy, he's a dead person. But I make myself grab his ankles and bring his feet back up, holding onto his knees because he's flopping all over the place.

Meeker has his elbows on the steering wheel and he's gazing through the front window. I'm beginning to feel very strange, hot and sweaty, and suddenly I can't breathe. I roll down the window because I have to get air in here or I'll suffocate, but Meeker turns and says sharply, "Put that up."

Instead I stick my face out, pulling in great gulps of the cool air that still holds the hot smells of the cars that drove this way today. I don't want to come back inside but I have to. I roll up the window.

Meeker's still staring out at the empty boulevard, drumming his fingers on the steering wheel and muttering to himself or to me. I hear him say, "That would work," but I'm not sure because my own thoughts are so loud I can't fix on anything be-hind them. What's going to happen? Will we go to jail? What have we done? Will we be blamed for Pidgy's death . . . but we didn't shoot him. We don't want him dead.

"If we take him home, his mother's going to have a heart attack," Meeker says softly. "When she gets her senses back, she'll start in with the questions."

I let my racing, muddled mind stop for a minute on Mrs. Glovsky. Husband dead. Son dead. Pidgy's three little sisters crying.

"The cops are going to be onto us," Meeker says in this soft, secret-agent kind of voice. 'You guys were with him,' they'll say. 'Tell us what happened and don't leave anything out.'"

"We weren't with him," I say. "I wish we had been. We'd have never let him go in that park." His legs are so heavy on me.

"We were with him earlier. But nobody knows that." Meeker has turned toward me and I can see his face, screwed up with concentration.

"Oh, Meek, what does it matter," I say.

"It does matter. If we think it through we can find a way out."

I've heard those words before, a lot. And I've al-ways listened. Because Meeker always *can* think his way out.

"Pidge didn't come to the party," Meek says. "We

went looking for him. He'd taken your mother's car without permission. You didn't know."

"I did," I say.

"You're not going to tell that part. We came home. We found the car all bashed up in your garage. Pidge had gone. That's all we know. He must have been walking around the street, freaked out over the accident, and somebody shot him. In this city people shoot people all the time. We found him."

"Are you going to start driving again, or am I?" I ask.

"Shut up and listen," Meeker says. "Pidge would like it if we could get ourselves out of this. You know that, Jase. What was the last thing he said? That he was sorry Pidge knew he'd screwed us up."

"*Pidge* had screwed us up?" I repeat. I can see the pale blur of Meeker's face, hear the sincerity in his voice.

"Sure he did. We were just about home free. You know what? If we'd been thinking straight we'd have left him in the park, called the cops anonymously. That would have been . . ."

I'm starting to shake and my teeth are clenched so tight my jaws ache.

"Wait, I've got it. Even better." Meeker's voice is suddenly alive with excitement. "We'll hide him."

"Hide him?" There's this strange coldness inside me, spreading, numbing.

"Yeah. That's it. We'll hide the body. We can drive up to . . . up to Griffith Park and find us a spot. There's plenty of underbrush up there. Nobody'll ever find him, at least not for a long time. It happens. You read about it."

Maybe Meek senses something in me. Some silent horror. He rushes on.

"We could bury him if you want. Get a spade. Your dad has one in the garage. And you could say something, like a priest. A prayer maybe."

A car whizzes past and Meeker doubles over so he's hidden. I think how quick he is. I think how many times he's hidden himself so he won't get caught. I think how many times I've let myself be hidden along with him. Maybe it takes a half minute for the lights to pass but it seems long as forever. It's like when you're drowning and all your life is supposed to pass before your eyes. I'm drowning now.

Meeker's sure I'll go along with him on this because he's the leader and I'm the follower and I always go along. Meek's sure, even though this is Pidgy lying on the seat.

Meeker's still squinched down but he's talking again, softly. "We'll have to do something about the blood in the car, but . . ."

I let Pidgy's feet slide and I lean forward and

grab the hair on top of Meeker's head and pull. He comes up fast.

"Hey!" he yelps and tries to jerk away, but I have a full-on grip.

"I could say something over his body like what?" I whisper. "Like, 'You always knew we'd leave you, Pidgy, and that's what we're doing. With any luck we'll get away with this the way we got away with everything else. Maybe the rats and the raccoons will get to you and you'll never turn up. That would be terrific. And your mom can keep searching for you and crying about you for the rest of her life.'" With every word I'm tugging harder on Meeker's hair. "'We're mad at you because you screwed things up.' You and I were his heroes. Did you know that, Meek? He loved us."

Meeker whams his head forward, gasps, and is free. He rubs at his scalp. I have a tuft of his hair, like a clump of bird feathers, in my hand. I try to drop it but my fingers are sticky with blood and the hairs cling. I rub them along Pidgy's pants.

Meeker wrenches open the door. "You stay then. I'm out of here. You take care of it. But don't try bringing me into it. I've been in bed all night. Harry and Babs know I came home early."

He has banged the door and I'm shouting inside the car and he probably can't even hear me.

"Your buddy Floyd saw you," I yell. "Don't try to lie your way out of this one, Meek."

He has heard me. "Don't worry about me. I'm good at lying."

I know he is. He has picked up a lot from his dad.

And then I'm sobbing and saying, "Pidgy, Pidgy," over and over. And Meeker's gone.

· · ·

A guy on a motorcycle drives past. I have the window on Pidgy's side open and I lean across him and yell, "Hey! We've had an accident here. A guy's hurt. Could you call the cops?"

The guy is wearing a white helmet and his head turns in my direction, then he guns his motor and hauls off. I'm not sure if he'll do it or not, so I get out and I lift Pidge's feet back onto the seat and make him as comfortable as I can. All the while I'm talking to him, telling him that I think maybe the best thing is if I just drive to the nearest police station, but that I'm not going to leave him. I'll be right there in the front seat. I'm just getting in behind the wheel when I hear sirens coming fast.

There's an ambulance and two police cars, their red lights flashing, and they're pulling in to the curb behind us.

I guess the motorcycle guy made the phone call after all.

CHAPTER 12

I'm home again from juvenile hall.

Pidge has been dead for three weeks and two days. He was buried in his red St. Jo's windbreaker and my dad said there were scads of kids from school at his funeral and at the memorial service after. He said there was some kind of petition to have Pidgy's football number, 52, retired the way they sometimes do in the pros when a big star dies, but the request was turned down. I guess they don't think it's right to do that much honor to someone who was killed trying to commit a robbery.

Meeker and I weren't allowed out of juvenile hall to go to the service. I lay on my bunk with my face to the wall, telling Pidge that I wouldn't have left him alone to be buried if I could have helped it, and I hope wherever he is he understands that.

I don't know what Meeker feels or thinks. We saw each other almost every day in juvie but we never spoke. Meeker had that same super-confident look. His smile said he knew secrets. His swagger told everyone he was special. It didn't take him long to have a following . . . three guys who strutted the way he strutted. I wondered which of his stories he'd laid on them and how many of them were lies. Big man in detention hall, I thought. It figures.

I'm home now. The judge released Meeker and me to the custody of our parents pending a hearing and I've had to live with my mom and dad's shock, and horror, and disbelief. They'd loved and trusted me. I know they still love me.

Meeker and I have not tried to see each other since we got back. We've been friends all our lives but we'll never be friends again.

Our dads met one day by accident in Blum's Drugstore.

"My kid's wild, but he's not bad," Harry told my dad. "What he *has* got is a lot of his old man's adventurous spirit."

Dad said Harry looked awful, shrunken and old. Dad doesn't seem to realize he's not looking too great himself.

I haven't told anyone that Meeker wanted to dump Pidge's body. Maybe that's another cover-up and I'm scared of cover-ups now. But telling wouldn't just reveal Meeker's true colors; somehow it would be another insult to Pidge's memory. I couldn't stand that. I did spill everything else, though. Every single thing.

Mom sold her Ford Fairlane. Floyd wanted to buy it but she wouldn't sell to him and I'm glad. She bought a small Honda. Our other car, the one Pidgy died in, is still impounded.

Yesterday my parents and I went to see his mom. However long I live, I hope I'll never have to do anything that hard. Mrs. Glovsky hugged me when I told her how terrible I felt about Pidgy.

"I loved him," I said.

She stroked my hair. "You think I don't know that, Jason? You think I don't know?"

Our hearing is next Thursday. My lawyer hopes I'll come out of it without doing more time in juvenile hall.

"The court should be lenient," he says. "You *were* the one who asked the guy to call the police and it wasn't you who robbed the Sunshine Market. It wasn't your dad's gun they found in the car."

They'd found Meeker's IOU, too, jammed in the glove compartment with all the money.

"What will happen to Meek?" I ask.

"He's in a lot more trouble than you are. Armed robbery is a serious offense. But Archie Fiscus is representing him and there's nobody better. Anyway, Mr. Meeker is not your worry."

That's true. But I can't forget that once Meek and I were friends.

My lawyer spreads his hands. "When it comes right down to it, neither of you boys killed anyone."

Maybe not. They haven't caught the guy yet, the one who shot Pidgy. But I'm not so sure who really killed him.

I haven't heard from Destiny. Why should I? We only had one real date and that doesn't make her my girl. Of course, even if she wanted to call she couldn't because we had so many crank calls we had to have our number changed. I thought about that and I got up my courage and called her. Her mom answered. "Yes? Can I tell her who it is?"

I hung up then because I was ashamed to say my name. It's pretty bad when you're ashamed to say your own name.

And then in today's mail I got a card, just a plain card with a deep red border, addressed to me.

It said: "I'm so sorry about Pidge. Maybe you and I can see each other some time. Destiny."

The writing was round and full and strong like Destiny herself. I held it to my face before I slid it gently under my pillow.

Mom told me Destiny was at Pidge's funeral.

"Someone said Meeker's girl was there, too, and the one Pidge was taking out that night — " her voice blurred.

Valerie. The girl from Radio Shack.

"Destiny put something in the casket with Pidge," Mom went on. "It was some kind of glass flower, very beautiful."

I turned my face away. The crystal rose!

"It's so pretty," Pidgy had said. "I wish I had one just like it."

I don't know what will happen to Meeker and me. The newspapers are still running the story. We're juveniles so they don't use our names. We're the "two classmates from St. Jo's." "Such nice kids," the neighbors call us when they're interviewed by reporters. We're "boys from good homes who made an error in judgment that escalated into a tragedy." It doesn't sound like much, worded like that. The stories don't say how one wrong move can lead to another and another and how in the end somebody can die.

"Whatever happens, I'll never get over this," I tell Rick, the counselor my parents got for me.

"You never will get over it all the way," he says. "But you'll grow from it. And learn."

I hope so.

I hope there'll be nights when I can sleep. When I don't lie, cold and scared, clutching Destiny's card and thinking of Pidge in his red St. Jo's jacket . . . Pidgy, down in the deep dark with the crystal rose.